CALLED TOGETHER

CALLED TOGETHER

STEVE AND MARY PROKOPCHAK

A
JANET
THOMA
BOOK

THOMAS NELSON PUBLISHERS
Nashville

Published in Nashville, Tennessee, by Janet Thoma Books, a division of Thomas Nelson,
Inc., Publishers, and distributed in Canada by Word Communications, Ltd., Richmond,
British Columbia, and in the United Kingdom by Word (UK), Ltd., Milton Keynes,
England.

Library of Congress

Printed in the United States of America

1 2 3 4 5 6 -99 98 97 96 95 94

*This premarital training manual is dedicated
first to the author of marriage,
our Lord Jesus Christ,
and secondly, to our children,
Joshua, Marc, and Brooke,
wonderful blessings from our call together.*

Contents

Foreword

During 1970, my wife, LaVerne, and I had the privilege of ministering to hundreds of young people each week. It was a sheer joy witnessing the grace of God in these young lives. They were young radicals who had chosen to give their all to build the kingdom of God. Eventually, these young men and women began to establish meaningful relationships. The next step was marriage.

In 1980, we obeyed the Lord's call to pioneer a new church filled with many of these same young people. We tried our best to teach them practical biblical principles to properly prepare them for this massive step: two becoming one in "holy matrimony." In retrospect, the instruction that was being given to these young couples during those days was "weighed in the scales and found wanting."

Steve Prokopchak joined our ministry team in 1987 and began to develop a counseling ministry for this new church. I was impressed with Steve's ability to trust the Word of God and the Holy Spirit as he gave clear biblical and practical counseling. He spoke into people's lives with compassion. After four years of writing and rewriting, *Called Together* emerged. The results have been tremendous!

A practical, insightful, and helpful book, *Called Together* has revolutionized premarital and postmarital counseling in our congregation. We have seen these scriptural principles worked out in the lives of the authors and in hundreds of engaged and married couples. And with its clear biblical approach, it helps engaged couples come face-to-face with real issues that they will confront throughout their lives together.

Throughout the past few years, requests for the *Called Together* materials have come from five continents of the world. Not only have these materials been used by pastors and counselors throughout North America, but materials have also been sent to Europe, Africa, South America, and New Zealand.

Thank you, Steve and Mary, for allowing the Lord to use you to help prepare engaged couples for marriage in a way that is scriptural and down-to-earth. May our Lord Jesus Christ be praised!

Larry and LaVerne Kreider
Senior Pastors
DOVE Christian Fellowship
Ephrata, Pennsylvania

Preface

Marriage is God's idea. He established it from the beginning. He has even based His relationship with the New Testament church upon the principles of marriage (Eph. 5:22–33). It is our desire to see couples trained to the honor and glory of God. We believe that the results of this training will validate our reasons for offering this course of study.

This manual is to be provocative by nature. It is designed to challenge you into whole-hearted, Christ-centered commitment or to cause you to rethink your decision for marriage. *Called Together* is best facilitated couple to couple—a counselor couple with a premarital couple.

We would like to present to you six reasons for premarital education: (1) maintaining a realistic perspective during the engagement period; (2) developing marital skills; (3) provoking serious thought concerning a lifelong commitment; (4) preventing problems in the future; (5) assessing the present relationship; (6) developing goals and long-term vision for the covenant relationship.

The home is the basic unit of the kingdom of God. As the home is established and restored, so will the kingdom of God be established and restored. We desire to see the kingdom of God established in every nation. This long-term vision will unfold as men and women of God—as families—are called together and then are called to go to the uttermost parts of the earth.

This course is for you if you are engaged to be married, if you are planning marriage someday, or if you are newly married.

Congratulations!

Congratulations to the two of you in your desire to spend your lives together serving God.

We appreciate your willingness to involve yourselves in premarital education. This course is designed to prepare you for God's call to marriage. These will be some of the most important counseling sessions you will ever be involved in. Marriage preparation counseling must be a time of thorough searching and communication concerning your past, present, and your dreams for the future.

In preparation for your first session, please carefully and prayerfully complete the following items: Premarital Counseling Information, Spiritual Overview, About Me, and A Biblical Concept of Love. A Biblical Concept of Love, is the only assignment you will work on together. You can complete the assignment Who I Am in Christ, at your own pace.

Please take all of your assignments seriously, complete them thoroughly, and turn them in to your counselors before each session. This will aid your counselors and help you complete the counseling process smoothly.

Even before this process is complete, you will see an improvement in the quality of your relationship. After you are married you will understand more fully the purpose of preparing for marriage by building a thorough foundation building.

Expect a meaningful experience. Be prepared for loving, honest, and challenging counselors. Do not hesitate to ask relevant questions of your fiancé and your counselors.

God bless you in your call together!

Counseling Schedule

Use this schedule to plan and to keep a record of your counseling appointments.

Session	Date	Time	Place
1			
2			
3			
4			
5			
6			

Premarital Counseling

Identification Data

Name _____

Address _____

City _____ State_____ Zip Code _____

Phone (Home)_____ Phone (Business)_____

Occupation_____

Sex_____ Birth Date_____

Premarital Status: Single_____ Separated_____

Divorced _____ Widowed_____

Education (Circle last year completed)   High School 8 9 10 11 12

College 1 2 3 4 5 6 +

Church Affiliation _____

Health Information

Rate your physical health:

Very good_____ Good_____ Average____ Declining____ Other _____

Your approximate weight_____ lbs.

Recent weight changes: Lost_____ Gained_____

List important present or past illnesses:_____

_____

Date of last medical exam:_____

Your physician _____

Address _____

Have you used drugs for other than medical purposes? Yes_____ No_____

Are you presently taking medication? Yes_____ No ____

Have you ever had a severe emotional upset?_____

Have you ever had any psychotherapy or individual counseling? Yes____ No ___

Have you ever had an abortion? Yes____ No ____

Religious Background

Do you consider yourself a Christian? Yes____ No ____

If yes, when were you saved?_____

Do you have a regular devotional time? Yes____ No ____

Are you engaging in family or individual worship/devotions? Yes ____ No____

Explain any recent changes or problems with your spiritual walk.

_____

_____

Personality

Have you ever suffered from depression? Yes_____ No_____

If yes, when?_____

Have you ever been involved in a cult, the occult, astrology, etc.? Yes ___ No __

Explain _____

_____

Do you fear anything? (e.g., are you afraid of the dark, heights, etc.?)

_____

Marriage Information

(If previously married)

How long did you know your former spouse before marriage? _____

Length of engagement _____

How did the separation occur? _____

Did you receive premarital instruction? Yes____ No ____

Children:

Name _____ Age ___ Sex____ Living with you? Yes ___ No____

Name _____ Age ___ Sex____ Living with you? Yes ___ No____

Name _____ Age ___ Sex____ Living with you? Yes ___ No____

Parental History

Were you raised by your natural parents? Yes _____ No____

Are your parents still living? Yes____ No _____

What is (was) your parents' religious affiliation? (e.g., Methodist, Catholic, etc.)

_____

Are (were) they Christians? Yes _____ No_____

Are your parents still living together? Yes____ No_____

If your parents are separated or divorced, when did this occur?

_____

Rate your parents' marriage: Happy____ Average____ Unhappy_____

As a child, did you feel closest to your: Father____ Mother____ Other ____?

Was your childhood: Happy____ Average_____ Unhappy ___?

How many brothers and sisters do you have? Brothers_____ Sisters_____

What number child were you? (first, middle, last)_____

Other

Is there any other information you feel is important?

Important: Please elaborate on any areas concerning premarital education that you would like to see covered.

Before You Marry

About Me

Premarital Session One

Taking an honest and intimate look at yourself and your partner is fundamental to the development and maintenance of unity within your marriage relationship. This session will challenge you to explore and understand yourself more fully.

When you and your partner come together in Session One with your premarital counselors, you will be given the opportunity to share about yourself and listen to your partner. Understanding one another will be a continuing process during your marriage relationship. Some of the most important foundational material, will be discussed in this session. Speak truthfully and listen intently.

We encourage you to be honest as you answer the following questions and complete the open-ended statements. Allow this first session to be a meaningful experience for you and your fiancé.

About Me

Complete the following open-ended statements with what first comes to mind. Do this exercise separately.

1. I see myself as _____

   _____

2. A word that would best describe me is_____

   _____

3. Success in life to me is _____

   _____

4. My strongest quality is_____

   _____

5. One of my weaknesses is _____

   _____

6. Others view me as _____

   _____

7. I become quiet when_____

   _____

8. When others have a different opinion than I do, my reaction is to _____

   _____

9. My feelings tend to be hurt when _____

   _____

10. I feel guilty when _____

_____

11. I worry when _____

_____

12. What makes me feel inadequate is _____

_____

13. I feel depressed when _____

_____

14. I am disappointed when _____

_____

15. My self-confidence falters when _____

_____

16. I get defensive when _____

_____

17. I get angry when _____

_____

18. When angry with someone, I tend to _____

_____

19. I feel trapped when _____

_____

20. I am afraid when _____

_____

Spiritual Overview

Complete the following statements concerning your spiritual life without the assistance of your fiancé.

1. My relationship with Jesus Christ is _____

   _____

   _____

   _____

2. My definition of *sin* is _____

   _____

   _____

   _____

3. Describe how you deal with sin. _____

   _____

   _____

4. Is Jesus Lord of your life? Please elaborate. _____

   _____

   _____

5. Have you been water baptized since accepting Christ? Yes_____ No_____

   If no, why not? _____

   Be prepared to share your experience.

6. As a believer, what is your experience with the Holy Spirit? _____

_____

_____

7. Describe your prayer life (where? when? why? etc.). _____

_____

_____

8. I read the Bible (when? for what reasons? etc.) _____

_____

_____

9. My personal commitment to attending a church (body of believers) is

(how often? for what reasons? etc.) _____

_____

_____

10. My understanding of God is_____

_____

_____

11. In a spiritual sense, marriage will solve the following problems: _____

_____

_____

12. I would like to make the following change(s) in my own spiritual life:

_____

_____

Biblical Concept of Love

The following scripture references, along with a word study on the three types of love, will provide an overview of the basic ingredient in healthy family relationships. Take the necessary time to read and study this exercise with your fiancé.

Agape—A self-giving love that does not seek anything in return. It's a love that endures even when another person becomes unlovable. It is like God's love, self-sacrificing and other-centered.

Phileo—A brotherly—friendship—companionship—type of love. *Phileo* denotes mutual attraction, cooperation, and communication between two individuals.

Eros—A love that seeks its own. Unlike agape love, it is self-centered, sensual, and inspired by selfish human nature. It is conditional love.

Scriptural study of love:

Matthew 22:37–39	Love God first
Luke 6:27–35	Love your enemies
John 13:34	Love one another
Romans 13:8–10	Love is the fulfillment of the law
1 Corinthians 8:1	Love edifies
Galatians 5:13	Serve through love
Galatians 6:2	Bear one another's burdens
Ephesians 4:2	Bear with one another in love
Ephesians 5:25	Husbands love as Christ loved
1 Peter 4:8	Love covers sins
1 John 3:16–18	Love is laying down your life
1 Corinthians 13	A more excellent way

Who I Am in Christ

First Thessalonians 5:33 states that we are spirit, soul, and body. Normally, we feed the body three meals a day. The soul is educated and fed emotionally. This exercise is designed to nourish the spirit, that part of us in which God dwells. Study the following scriptures together and individually to discover who you are in Christ.

I am now God's child 1John 3:2
I am born of the incorruptible seed of God's Word ....1 Peter 1:23
I am loved by Christ ....Revelation 1:5
I am forgiven all my sins ....Ephesians 1:7
I am justified from all things...Acts 13:39
I am the righteousness of God ....2 Corinthians 5:21
I am free from all condemnation...Romans 8:1
I can forget the past ....Philippians 3:13
I am a new creature ....2 Corinthians 5:17
I am the temple of the Holy Spirit...1 Corinthians 6:19
I am redeemed from the curse of the law..................................Galatians 3:13
I am accepted in Christ ....Ephesians 1:6
I am reconciled to God ....2 Corinthians 5:18
I am beloved of God..1 John 4:10
I am a saint...Romans 1:7
I am holy and without blame before Him ....Ephesians 1:4
I am the head and not the tail...Deuteronomy 28:13
I am called of God...2 Timothy 1:9
I am brought near by the blood of Christ...................................Ephesians 2:13
I am complete in Christ...Colossians 2:10
I am delivered from the power of darkness ....Colossians 1:13
I am an ambassador for Christ...2 Corinthians 5:20
I am the salt of the earth ....Matthew 5:13
I am the light of the world ....Matthew 5:14
I am dead to sin ....Romans 6:2
I am alive to God ....Romans 6:11
I am raised up with Christ and seated in heavenly places............Ephesians 2:6
I am a king and a priest to God...Revelation 1:6

I am loved with an everlasting love ....Jeremiah 31:3

I am fit to partake of His inheritance.....................................Colossians 1:12

I am an heir of God and a joint-heir with Christ ....Romans 8:17

I am more than a conqueror...Romans 8:37

I am healed by the wounds of Jesus..1 Peter 2:24

I am built on the foundation of the apostles and prophets,
    with Jesus Christ Himself as the chief cornerstone ....Ephesians 2:20

I am in Christ Jesus by God's act ....1 Corinthians 1:30

I am kept by God's power...1 Peter 1:5

I am sealed with the promised Holy Spirit...............................Ephesians 1:13

I have everlasting life ....John 5:24

I am crucified with Christ ....Galatians 2:20

I am a partaker of the divine nature...2 Peter 1:4

I have been given all things that pertain to life.............................2 Peter 1:3

I have been blessed with every spiritual blessing ....Ephesians 1:3

I have peace with God...Romans 5:1

I proclaim God's praise ....1 Peter 2:9

I can do all things through Christ...Philippians 4:13

I have all my needs met by God according to His
    riches in glory in Christ Jesus...Philippians 4:19

I shall do even greater works than Christ Jesus...........................John 14:12

I am confirmed to the end ....1 Corinthians 1:8

I am elected...1 Thessalonians 1:4

I overcome the world ....1 John 5:4

I have a guaranteed inheritance ....Ephesians 1:14

I am a fellow citizen with the saints...Ephesians 2:19

I am free ....John 8:36

I always triumph in Christ...2 Corinthians 2:14

I am in Jesus Christ's hands ....John 10:28

Christ in me is the hope of glory..Colossians 1:27

About Us

Many couples enter marriage unrealistically. God wants us to be full of faith but "wise as serpents." With the great wealth of literature, videos and tapes available to us on the subjects of marriage, sex, finances, communication, etc., no couple should enter marriage unaware of Satan's devices to undermine and destroy relationships.

Why do you want to marry this particular person? How do you and your fiancé know that God is calling you together? What are your expectations for this marriage? How would you react to potentially difficult circumstances should they arise during your marriage? Are your parents in agreement with your engagement? Assignments for Session Two address these questions. This session will also help you to assess your expectations and perceptions of marriage.

God has a perfect design for marriage. When conflicts or difficult circumstances arise, God's Word offers help and hope for each situation.

Reasons for Marriage

1. Have you thought through your reasons for marrying your fiancé? Take the time to list ten of those reasons.

    1. _____

       _____

       _____

    2. _____

       _____

       _____

    3. _____

       _____

       _____

    4. _____

       _____

       _____

    5. _____

       _____

       _____

    6. _____

       _____

       _____

7. _____

_____

_____

8. _____

_____

_____

9. _____

_____

_____

10.

_____

_____

2. What confirmation do you and your fiancé have that God is calling you together? Please elaborate.

Expectations and Perceptions of Marriage

Without the help of your fiancé, list ten expectations you will have of your fiancé when you are married. For example, a husband might expect his wife to never be employed outside the home, to balance the checkbook, to mow the lawn, or to perform all household duties. A wife might expect her husband to be the head of the family, to administer all child discipline, to help with housework, or to decrease sports activities with his friends.

1. _____

_____

_____

2. _____

_____

_____

3. _____

_____

_____

4. _____

_____

_____

5. _____

_____

_____

6. _____

_____

_____

7. _____

_____

_____

8. _____

_____

_____

9. _____

_____

_____

10.

_____

_____

Reactions

How would you react to the following circumstances?

1. You and your spouse are scheduled to work opposite shifts._____

_____

2. You discover that your spouse is attracted to someone else. _____

_____

3. Your spouse no longer has time for daily devotions. _____

_____

_____

4. A friend becomes flirtatious with your spouse._____

_____

5. You cannot get along with your sister-in-law. _____

_____

6. You have a communication problem with your mother-in-law. _____

_____

_____

7. You have difficulty becoming pregnant. _____

_____

_____

8. Your apartment is too small and you cannot afford a larger one. _____

_____

_____

9. Your spouse spends more money on himself/herself than on you. _____

_____

_____

10. You discover your spouse has incurred significant credit card debt. _____

_____

_____

11. Your spouse is laid off from his/her job. _____

_____

12. Your sex life is less than exciting. _____

_____

13. Communication becomes increasingly difficult. _____

_____

14. You discover that your spouse cannot let go of his/her mother. _____

_____

_____

15. A job change requires you and your spouse to move to the other side of the country. _____

_____

16. You find yourself battling attraction to a coworker. _____

_____

_____

Our Parents

Families of origin play a vital role when two persons are considering a lifetime together. Discuss your feelings about your parents and your future in-laws by answering the following questions.

1. Have you communicated to your parents your desire to be married? ____

   _____

2. Are your father and mother in agreement with your plans for marriage?

   _____

3. Do your parents agree with the length of your engagement and the date

   of the wedding? _____

   _____

4. Have your parents expressed any hesitations concerning your desire to be

   married?_____

   _____

5. Have your parents met your fiancé's parents?_____

6. Do you feel your parents are supportive of the person you want to

   marry? _____

7. Are your parents Christians? _____

   If not, how will that affect your relationship now or after you are married? _____

   _____

   _____

8. Will you attend your parents' church or another? _____

9. Have you asked your parents for any wisdom or advice that they may have for you?_____

   If so, what advice have they shared with you?_____

   _____

10. How can you maintain a spirit of honor towards your parents during your engagement? _____

    _____

    _____

11. How can you maintain a spirit of honor towards your parents after you are married? _____

    _____

    _____

12. How often do you plan to visit your parents after you are married? _____

    _____

13. How will you respond to advice from your parents that you don't agree with? _____

    _____

14. Are there other matters concerning your parents or your fiancé's parents that you would have questions about?_____

    _____

    _____

Marriage: God's Design

Review individually and then with your premarital counselors.

1. Genesis 1:27
   - Male and female was God's idea.
   - Creation was incomplete without woman.
   - The world would be one-dimensional with only one sex.

2. Genesis 2:18–22
   - God's design was to meet the first problem of the human race: loneliness.
   - Woman was taken from man to complement him.
   - Woman was totally suitable—spiritually, intellectually, emotionally, and physically—to man.
   - She was designed as a "helper" (aid or support to a friend or ally).
   - A husband and wife will still be lonely if their spiritual, intellectual, emotional, and physical needs are not met.

3. Genesis 2:23
   - Marriage was planned to bring happiness, not misery.
   - "Bone of my bones, flesh of my flesh" describes a joyous, intimate, personal relationship.
   - Adam was expressing his joy over woman. She completed him and took away his loneliness because he now had a companion like himself—"One who is as my own flesh!"

4. Genesis 2:24
   - Marriage begins with a leaving of other relationships.
   - Man and woman leave the closest of relationships (father, mother) to establish a new household that they will be responsible for, no longer being under parental authority. Rather than looking to others to meet their needs, they now focus on each other (other things—business, career, house, hobbies, talents, interests, church work—hold lesser priority).

5. Genesis 2:24
   - Marriage is joining throughout your lifetime, "cleaving."
   - Don't "leave" unless you desire to "cleave."

- To cleave is to adhere, to stick, to be attached by a strong tie.
- The husband is primarily responsible to do all he can do to form inseparable ties with his wife. The wife must then respond in the same manner.
- Cleaving is a wholehearted commitment in the intellectual, emotional, spiritual, and physical aspects of relationships.
- Anything that puts distance between husband and wife should be avoided.
- Cleaving involves two characteristics:
    1. Unswerving loyalty
    2. An active, pursuing love that will not let go
        To test whether an action, attitude, word, or decision will help you cleave ask the following questions:
        - Will this draw us closer or drive us apart?
        - Will it build our relationship or tear it down?
        - Will it bring about a positive response or a negative response?
        - Does it express my love and loyalty to my partner or does it reveal my self-centered individualism?

6. Genesis 2:24–25
    - Marriage means oneness: Two shall become one! Marriage must then be monogamous (two people only). No adultery or promiscuity. (See Prov. 6:32.)
    - Marriage must be heterosexual. One woman for one man.
    - Becoming one involves sexual union. (See Gen. 4:1; Eph. 5:31–32.)

Note: Marriage is two individuals merging into one. This is why divorce is so devastating. There are not two people left, but two fractions of one.

Adapted from *Love Life for Every Married Couple* by Ed Wheat, M.D. Copyright © 1980, 1987 by Ed Wheat, M.D. Used by permission of Zondervan Publishing House, Grand Rapids, Michigan.

Let's Talk

An effective communication system is vital to a stable, intimate, and satisfying marriage relationship. A breakdown of communication is almost always a primary cause of marital dysfunction. Ed Cole, author of *Communication, Sex, and Money*, states that when communication stops, abnormality sets in, and the ultimate end of abnormality is death of the relationship. Just as faith dies when we refuse to communicate with our heavenly Father, so will a marriage die when a couple refuses to communicate. Ephesians 4:29–30 reveals to us that communication should edify, not corrupt. The Holy Spirit is grieved when we are not ministers of grace.

Our communication goals are to share with one another freely; to be lovingly honest about what we think and feel; to understand each other; to listen respectfully and respond appropriately; to be able to disagree and discuss our disagreements without becoming hurt or attacking one another; to have conversation that is beneficial and uplifting. We will work toward these communication goals through varied homework assignments including nonverbal communication, communication guidelines, effective communication, and scenario communication.

Norm Wright, a well-known marriage counselor, states in his book *Training Christians to Counsel* that communication can be broken down as follows:

> 7% words (content)
> 38% attitude (tone of voice)
> 55% body language

Take this opportunity to begin to analyze your personal communication tendencies. What body language do you display when you are angry, hurt, or selfish? Under what circumstances does your tone of voice change? Even if you feel communication is one of your strong points, give full attention to the assignments which follow. Scripture has a lot to say about the way we talk to each other. Be open to discovering some hindrances to good communication in your life.

Nonverbal Communication

1. List at least five ways in which you have experienced nonverbal communication from your fiancé (both positive and negative).

   1. _____

   2. _____

   3. _____

   4. _____

   5. _____

2. Share several experiences you have had concerning attitude and tone of voice while communicating with your fiancé. (Again, share at least one positive and one negative experience.)

   1. _____

   2. _____

3. Identify any factors that have hindered communication for you and your fiancé (for example: in-laws, past relationships, beliefs, etc.).

   1. _____

   2. _____

   3. _____

   4. _____

   5. _____

4. Study the following scripture verses and record what they reveal to you concerning nonverbal communication.

   Genesis 3:7–10 _____

   _____

Genesis 4:5–6 _____

_____

Genesis 40:6–7 _____

_____

Joshua 7:6 _____

_____

1 Samuel 18:4 _____

_____

1 Kings 19:3–4*a* _____

_____

1 Kings 21:4 _____

_____

Proverbs 31:12–27 _____

_____

Mark 2:3–5 _____

_____

Luke 18:10–13 _____

_____

1 John 3:17–18 _____

_____

How Do We Talk Together?

What kind of interaction do you and your fiancé have with each other? Respond to the statements below by placing a check under the answer that best describes you and your fiancé.

	Always	Usually	Sometimes	Rarely	Never
1. I listen to my fiancé.					
2. My fiancé listens to me.					
3. I understand what my fiancé is trying to say.					
4. My fiancé understands what I am trying to say.					
5. I show appreciation when my fiancé does things for me.					
6. My fiancé shows appreciation when I do things for him/her.					
7. I show interest in my fiancé's ideas, thoughts, feelings, and activities.					
8. My fiancé shows interest in my ideas, thoughts, feelings, and activities.					
9. I feel comfortable disagreeing with what my fiancé says.					
10. I feel comfortable when my fiancé disagrees with me.					
11. I show interest in facts and information.					
12. My fiancé shows interest in facts and information.					
13. I am able to express feelings and emotions.					
14. My fiancé is able to express feelings and emotions.					
15. I am happy to just share and spend time with my fiancé.					

Communication Guidelines

Think about the following guidelines and study the supporting scripture verses.

Part A:

1. Be a ready listener, and do not answer until the other person has finished talking (Prov. 18:13; James 1:19).

2. Be slow to speak. Think first. Don't be hasty in your words. Speak in such a way that the other person can understand and accept what you say (Prov. 15:23; 29:20; James 1:19).

3. Don't go to bed angry! Each day, clear the offenses of that day. Speak the truth, but do it in love. Do not exaggerate (Eph. 4:15, 25–26).

4. Do not use silence to frustrate the other person. Explain why you are hesitant to talk at this time (Prov. 10:19; 15:28; 16:21, 23; 18:2).

5. Do not become involved in quarrels. It is possible to disagree without quarreling (Prov. 17:14; 20:3; Eph. 4:31).

6. Do not respond in uncontrolled anger. Use a kind response and a soft tone of voice (Prov. 14:29; 15:1; 25:15; 29:11; Eph. 4:26–31).

7. When you are wrong, admit it, ask for forgiveness, and then ask how you can change (Prov. 12:15; 16:2; 20:6; 21:2; Matt. 5:23–25; James 5:16).

8. When someone confesses a wrong to you, tell that person you forgive him/her. Be sure it is forgiven and not brought up again to the person, to others, or to yourself (Luke 17:3–4; Eph. 4:32; Col. 3:13).

9. Avoid nagging (Prov. 10:19; 16:21, 23; 17:9; 18:6–7; 21:19; 27:15).

10. Do not blame or criticize the other person. Instead, restore, encourage, and edify (Rom. 14:13; Gal. 6:1; 1 Thess. 5:11).

11. If someone verbally attacks, criticizes, or blames you, do not respond in the same manner (Rom. 12:17, 21; 1 Peter 2:23; 3:9).

12. Try to understand the other person's opinion. Make allowances for differences (Eph. 4:2; Phil. 2:1–3).

13. Be concerned about the other person's interests (Phil. 2:4).

Part B:

1. What attitudes or messages do the following sentences convey to you? Do they convey respect, appreciation, consideration, encouragement, affection, and love—or disdain, disrespect, rudeness, animosity, hostility, and rejection? Try to imagine yourself hearing these sentences from someone else.

   "You don't really care." _____

   _____

   "I really need you." _____

   _____

   "Well, what do you have to complain about today?" _____

   _____

   _____

   "It sounds like you had a difficult day. Is there any way I can help you?"

   _____

   _____

   "You shouldn't feel that way!" _____

   _____

   _____

"I'm really sorry that you feel that way. How can I help? I'll be glad to pray for you and do anything I can." _____

_____

"You never kiss me." _____

_____

"Do you know what, honey? I really love you and like to have you hold me and kiss me." _____

_____

"Well, what do you know? Miracles still happen. You're ready on time."

_____

_____

"Hey, hon, I just wanted you to know that I really appreciated the way you hurried to be ready to go on time." _____

_____

_____

"Honey, you're terrific, and getting better all the time." _____

_____

_____

"You always forget what I ask you to do." _____

_____

_____

"I like the way you smile. It really brightens my day." _____

_____

_____

"We ought to have company more often. It's the only time we get good food around here." _____

_____

_____

"That was a super meal. You are a fantastic cook." _____

_____

_____

"How come you could get home early tonight when you don't do it other nights?" _____

_____

_____

"Boy, it's really great you got home early. I really miss you during the day." _____

_____

_____

Adapted from *A Homework Manual for Biblical Counseling, Volume 1* by Wayne Mack. Copyright © 1979. Used by permission of Presbyterian and Reformed Publishing Company, Phillipsburg, New Jersey.

How to Become an Effective Communicator

A. The following scriptures discuss hindrances to good communication. As you study them, record the hindrances in the blank provided. Number one has been completed as an example.

1. Ephesians 4:25 *Stop lying and speak the truth*

2. Ephesians 4:29 _____

3. Ephesians 4:31 _____

4. Colossians 3:8 _____

5. Colossians 3:9 _____

6. Proverbs 11:12 _____

7. Proverbs 11:13 _____

8. Proverbs 12:16 _____

9. Proverbs 12:18 _____

10. Proverbs 15:1 _____

11. Proverbs 15:5 _____

12. Proverbs 16:27 _____

13. Proverbs 17:9 _____

14. Proverbs 18:2 _____

15. Proverbs 18:6 _____

16. Proverbs 18:8 _____

17. Proverbs 18:13 _____

18. Proverbs 18:17 _____

19. Proverbs 18:23 _____

20. Proverbs 19:1 _____

21. Proverbs 19:5 _____

22. Proverbs 20:19 _____

23. Proverbs 20:25 _____

24. Proverbs 25:24 _____

25. Proverbs 26:18–19_____

26. Proverbs 26:20–21_____

27. Proverbs 26:22 _____

28. Proverbs 28:2 _____

29. Proverbs 29:20 _____

30. Proverbs 29:21 _____

B. Examine your effectiveness as a communicator. What hindrances to good communication need to be eliminated from your life?

1. _____

2. _____

3. _____

4. _____

5. _____

6. _____

7. _____

8. _____

8. _____

9. _____

Adapted from *A Homework Manual for Biblical Counseling*, *Volume 1* by Wayne Mack. Copyright © 1979. Used by permission of Presbyterian and Reformed Publishing Company, Phillipsburg, New Jersey.

Do You Discuss . . . ?

Do you and your fiancé discuss:

	Yes	No	Sometimes
1. your feelings and attitudes?	____	____	____
2. your differences?	____	____	____
3. your hurts?	____	____	____
4. plans that involve both of you?	____	____	____
5. one another's faults?	____	____	____
6. one another's families?	____	____	____
7. your criticisms of one another?	____	____	____
8. things you have noticed concerning your relationship but are afraid to talk about?	____	____	____
9. jealousy you may have of one another?	____	____	____
10. disagreements without losing your temper?	____	____	____
11. how you will manage your money?	____	____	____
12. your expectations of one another in parenting?	____	____	____
13. your views on training children?	____	____	____
14. matters when one of you is quiet or sulking?	____	____	____
15. your physical boundaries while engaged?	____	____	____

Scenario Communication

Please indicate how you will respond in the following situations.

1. You have just arrived home from work. You are recounting an important conversation with your boss. Right in the middle of it your spouse asks, "Did you bring the mail in?"

2. You are mowing the yard. Your spouse asks you to go to the store for some milk, but you really want to finish mowing.

3. It has been over a week since the clothes were washed. You are out of socks.

4. You have had another heated discussion about your finances. Your spouse has purchased a non-budgeted item again.

5. You notice that whenever you have something important or confrontational to discuss with your spouse, he or she yawns and seems disinterested.

Finances

Agreement is basic in successful marriages. "Can two walk together, unless they are agreed?" (Amos 3:3). Financial agreement is an important marital goal. When partners agree on getting out of debt, tithing, overcoming a financial crisis, or being better stewards, then the power of God is released to work in their lives.

God's Word offers clear guidelines and principles for handling money. A scriptural overview of finances is included in this session. You will also have opportunity to express your personal financial views, to describe your financial background, to complete a cost estimation exercise, and to work on a budget profile.

God wants you to have a strategy for financial health. Discover a place of agreement and you will discover a place of blessing and provision.

Personal Financial Views

In order to discover and provide clarification on your personal financial views, answer the following questions without the help of your fiancé.

1. Will you have joint or separate checking accounts? _____

2. Who will do the bookkeeping? _____

3. Who will write the checks when paying bills? _____

4. Will you buy or rent a home? If renting, how soon do you expect to buy?

   _____

5. How often will you go out to dinner? _____

6. Will you maintain a monthly budget? _____

7. Will you use credit cards or borrow money? _____

8. Will you buy a car with borrowed money? _____

9. What percentage of your paycheck should be saved each month? _____

10. Will you tithe and give offerings? _____

11. Will the wife return to work after you have children? _____

12. What insurance(s) will you purchase? _____

13. Who will be responsible to make out a will? _____

14. How much freedom would you like to purchase items without your

    spouse's approval? _____

15. How much spending money will you and your spouse normally have in

    your possession? _____

Financial Background

Given the assumption that your parents' view towards money will have a profound effect on your views, discuss what you have observed about your parents' finances. Be prepared to share how your views are similar to or different from your parents' views of money.

1. Did your parents maintain a budget? _____

_____

2. Who was in charge of the finances? _____

_____

3. Were the bills paid on time? _____

_____

4. Were your parents generous with those in need? _____

_____

5. Did your parents agree or did they argue a lot concerning money? _____

_____

_____

6. Did they focus on the necessities or did they purchase a lot of luxuries?

_____

7. Did they take family vacations? _____

_____

8. Did one or both parents have a spending allowance? _____

_____

9. Did your parents place importance on saving their money? _____

_____

10. Did your parents tithe or support mission work? _____

_____

Cost Estimation

Do you have any idea of the cost of the items you'll need to maintain your household or your own physical well-being, i.e., food, clothes, tools for lawn-care and household repairs? Have fun and see how close you can come, without the help of your fiancé, to the estimated cost of the following items.

1. A five-pound ham _____
2. A pound of American cheese _____
3. A pound of ground turkey _____
4. A can of cherry pie filling _____
5. A five-pound bag of sugar _____
6. A man's sport coat _____
7. A woman's swimsuit _____
8. A pair of pantyhose _____
9. A skirt and blouse _____
10. A nylon slip _____
11. A bottle of fingernail polish _____
12. A pair of woman's shoes _____
13. A pair of man's slacks _____
14. A leather briefcase _____
15. A leather handbag _____
16. A haircut _____
17. A hair permanent _____

18. A tune-up for a V-6 engine _____
19. A case of motor oil _____
20. Front disc brakes _____
21. 100 pounds of lawn food _____
22. A six-foot wooden stepladder _____
23. A 22-inch mower _____
24. A gallon of latex paint _____
25. Queen-size no-iron sheets _____
26. Two pairs of window curtains _____
27. A set of bath towels _____
28. A newspaper subscription _____
29. A child's baseball mitt _____
30. A deer hunting rifle _____
31. Two tickets to a football game _____
32. Two tickets to a play _____
33. A fishing license _____
34. A round of golf _____

Scriptural Truths about Finances

Study the following passages together to discover how to acquire, how to regard, and how to spend money. Indicate the principles that you derive from each passage.

1. Deuteronomy 8:17–18 _____

_____

2. Proverbs 11:24–25 _____

_____

3. Proverbs 11:28 _____

_____

4. Proverbs 13:22 _____

_____

5. Proverbs 22:1, 4, 7 _____

_____

6. Ecclesiastes 5:10 _____

_____

7. Jeremiah 9:23–24 _____

_____

8. Matthew 6:19–21 _____

_____

9. Luke 12:13–21 _____

_____

10. Romans 13:6–8 _____

_____

11. 1 Timothy 6:3–10,17–18 _____

_____

12. Hebrews 13:5 _____

_____

The Personal Finances Budget Sheet

When two people come together in marriage, an entirely new financial picture is created; two incomes are merging into one. This presents potential conflict if the couple does not follow practical guidelines for managing money.

As you and your fiancé plan your proposed budget, use this budget sheet as a blueprint for your money management. Listing your assets and liabilities is good record keeping, and it will enable you and your counselors to "see" your spending plan, which in turn will help you to effectively control your expenditures. Use the finished product to establish financial goals and to set priorities.

Instructions

Record the known or estimated monthly dollar figure for each category on the budget sheet. (We've included two blank sheets for you.) The definitions of the categories are listed below to help you determine the scope of each one. The completed example on page 46 will serve as a guideline.

Tithe: List your regular support (tithe) to your church (anything over 10% may be listed under the *Giving* category).

Tax: List federal, state and county taxes.

Investment: List any money invested for future care of your family (IRA's, retirement programs, home savings, etc).

Mortgage/Rent: List mortgage payment or rent payment.

Housing Maintenance: If you own your home, estimate monthly maintenance costs.

Utilities: List your monthly utility costs.

Telephone: Estimate your monthly phone bill.

Food & Supplies: Include food (work and school lunches), drug store supplies, department store sundries (toiletries, laundry).

Clothing: Estimate a monthly budget.

Autos: List auto payment(s) and the cost of insurance, driver's licenses, vehicle registration, gas, and maintenance.

Medical/Dental: Include health insurance payments and money spent for medicines, medical/dental/optical checkups.

Gifts: List monthly expenses for gifts (birthday, wedding, etc.)

Stationery: Estimate the cost of postage and stationery.

Dining: List restaurant meals eaten out.

Travel/Vacation: List weekend travel and yearly vacation.

Recreation/Entertainment: List money spent for family activities and sporting events (swimming, bowling, movies, football games, etc).

Miscellaneous: List expenses not covered above, college loans, marriage seminars, periodical subscriptions, life insurance, and personal debt.

Giving: List missionary support and special offerings.

Savings: List money set aside for emergencies. Indicate withdrawals with brackets ( ).

When the monthly budget amounts are completed, compute the totals. First, work from left to right adding up annual totals for each category. The annual totals added together, excluding income, can be more than, equal to, or less than the total annual income. Figure the average monthly total for each category by dividing each annual total by twelve.

Personal Finances Budget Sheet Example

Category percentages that may be helpful in preparing a budget.

%	Category	January	February	March	April	May	June	July	August	September	October	November	December	Annual Total	Average Monthly Total
	Income Husband	1200	1200	1500*	1200	1200	1500*	1200	1200	1500*	1200	1200	1500*	15600	1300
	Wife	440	440	550*	440	440	550*	440	440	550*	440	440	550*	5720	477
10%	Tithe	164	164	205	164	164	205	164	164	205	164	164	205	2132	178
20%	Federal Tax 16.9%	277	277	346	277	277	346	277	277	346	277	277	346	3600	300
	State Tax 2.1%	35	35	43	35	35	43	35	35	43	35	35	43	452	38
	County Tax 1%	16	16	21	16	16	21	16	16	21	16	16	21	212	18
8%	Investment FICA	131	131	164	131	131	164	131	131	164	131	131	164	1704	142
	Mortgage	—	—	—	—	—	—	—	—	—	—	—	—	—	—
	Rent	350	350	350	350	350	350	350	350	350	350	350	350	4200	350
	Housing Maintenance	—	—	—	—	—	—	—	—	—	—	—	—	—	—
21%	Electricity	—	—	—	—	—	—	—	—	—	—	—	—	—	—
	Heat	—	—	—	—	—	—	—	—	—	—	—	—	—	—
	Water	—	—	—	—	—	—	—	—	—	—	—	—	—	—
	Sewer	—	—	—	—	—	—	—	—	—	—	—	—	—	—
	Disposal	—	—	—	—	—	—	—	—	—	—	—	—	—	—
11%	Telephone	23	23	23	23	23	23	23	23	23	23	23	23	276	23
	Food & Supplies	195	195	195	195	195	195	195	195	195	195	195	195	2340	195
2.2%	Clothing	40	40	40	40	40	40	40	40	40	40	40	40	480	40
	Auto Payment/Lease	—	—	—	—	—	—	—	—	—	—	—	—	—	—
9.9%	Auto Gas/Oil	68	68	68	68	68	68	68	68	68	68	68	68	816	68
	Auto Insurance	—	—	—	400	—	—	—	—	—	400	—	—	800	67
	Auto License/Reg.	—	—	—	—	—	50	—	—	—	—	—	—	50	4
	Auto Maintenance	40	40	40	40	40	40	40	40	40	40	40	40	480	40
2.5%	Medical/Dental	45	45	45	45	45	45	45	45	45	45	45	45	540	45
2%	Gifts	15	15	15	15	50	15	15	15	15	50	100	100	420	35
.5%	Stationery	8	8	8	8	8	8	8	8	8	8	8	8	96	8
3.1%	Dining	30	—	—	30	—	—	30	—	—	30	—	—	120	10
	Travel/Vacation	—	—	—	—	—	—	—	200	160	—	—	—	360	30
	Rec/Entertainment	15	15	15	15	15	15	15	15	15	15	15	15	180	15
6.7%	Miscellaneous	—	—	—	—	—	—	—	—	—	—	—	—	—	—
	Education	—	—	90	—	—	—	—	90	—	—	—	90	270	23
	Subscriptions	—	20	—	—	—	—	—	—	—	—	—	—	20	2
	Life Insurance	—	—	—	—	36	—	—	—	60	—	—	—	96	8
	Debt	—	—	—	—	—	—	1000	—	—	—	—	—	1000	—
1.1%	Giving Missionary	20	20	20	20	20	20	20	20	20	20	20	20	240	20
2%	Savings	168	178	362	<232>	127	402	<832>	<92>	232	<267>	113	277	436	35
	Cumulative Savings	168	346	708	476	603	1005	173	81	313	46	159	436		

Husband and wife are paid weekly on Fridays. *Indicates the months with 5 Fridays. Husband earns $7.50 per hour, 40 hours per week and the wife earns $5.50 per hour, 20 hours per week. They have no children.

Personal Finances Budget Sheet

Category percentages that may be helpful in preparing a budget.

	Category	January	February	March	April	May	June	July	August	September	October	November	December	Annual Total	Average Monthly Total
	Income														
10%	Tithe														
20%	Federal Tax 16.9%														
	State Tax 2.1%														
	County Tax 1%														
8%	Investment FICA														
	Mortgage														
	Rent														
	Housing Maintenance														
21%	Electricity														
	Heat														
	Water														
	Sewer														
	Disposal														
	Telephone														
11%	Food & Supplies														
2.2%	Clothing														
	Auto Payment/Lease														
9.9%	Auto Gas/Oil														
	Auto Insurance														
	Auto License/Reg.														
	Auto Maintenance														
2.5%	Medical/Dental														
2%	Gifts														
.5%	Stationery														
	Dining														
3.1%	Travel/Vacation														
	Rec/Entertainment														
6.7%	Miscellaneous														
	Education														
	Subscriptions														
	Life Insurance														
	Debt														
1.1%	Giving														
2%	Savings														
	Cumulative Savings														

Husband and wife are paid weekly on Fridays. *Indicates the months with 5 Fridays. Husband earns $7.50 per hour, 40 hours per week and the wife earns $5.50 per hour, 20 hours per week. They have no children.

Personal Finances Budget Sheet

Category percentages that may be helpful in preparing a budget.		Category	January	February	March	April	May	June	July	August	September	October	November	December	Annual Total	Average Monthly Total
		Income														
10%		Tithe														
20%		Federal Tax 16.9%														
		State Tax 2.1%														
		County Tax 1%														
8%		Investment FICA														
		Mortgage														
		Rent														
		Housing Maintenance														
21%		Electricity														
		Heat														
		Water														
		Sewer														
		Disposal														
		Telephone														
11%		Food & Supplies														
2.2%		Clothing														
		Auto Payment/Lease														
		Auto Gas/Oil														
9.9%		Auto Insurance														
		Auto License/Reg.														
		Auto Maintenance														
2.5%		Medical/Dental														
2%		Gifts														
.5%		Stationery														
		Dining														
3.1%		Travel/Vacation														
		Rec/Entertainment														
6.7%		Miscellaneous														
		Education														
		Subscriptions														
		Life Insurance														
		Debt														
1.1%		Giving														
2%		Savings														
		Cumulative Savings														

Husband and wife are paid weekly on Fridays. *Indicates the months with 5 Fridays. Husband earns $7.50 per hour, 40 hours per week and the wife earns $5.50 per hour, 20 hours per week. They have no children.

Sexual Relations

God is the creator of sex. He originated lovemaking between married partners. Sex is "a beautiful and intimate relationship shared uniquely by a husband and wife," as stated by Tim and Beverly LaHaye in their book *The Act of Marriage*.

In His Word, God has given much information and many directions about sexual relations. He does not consider sex an embarrassing topic. He addresses marriage in a discreet and wholesome way.

God wants you to go into marriage informed about and prepared for sexual relations. God's desire is that you anticipate and then enjoy this wonderful aspect of the marriage relationship. Videos, books, and audio tapes on the subject of sexual relationships are available to the church today and are authored by knowledgeable and dedicated Christians. Take advantage of the resources available to you to help you to understand God's intent for sexual relations.

Exercises will provide for you a scriptural look at sex in marriage, questions for discussion, an attitude and beliefs self-examination, and some practical information that will help you to become a caring and creative lover.

Finally, you will find helpful information about birth control in Appendix C and honeymoon precautions in Appendix D.

Sex in Marriage

A Look at the Scriptures

Express briefly, in your own words, what each of the following scriptures reveals concerning attitude, reproduction, communication, and sexual pleasure within the boundaries of marriage.

Genesis 2:24–25—What will leaving parents and being united to our spouse bring forth? _____

_____

Genesis 1:28; Deuteronomy 7:13–14; Psalm 127:3–5; 139:13–15—What is the blessing that physical oneness produces between a husband and wife?____

_____

_____

_____

Song of Solomon 4:1–12; Proverbs 5:15–21; 1 Corinthians 7:2–5—How is sexual pleasure a part of God's purpose for marriage?_____

_____

_____

_____

Hebrews 13:4; 1 Corinthians 6:12—Are there any limitations on sexual pleasure for a married couple? _____

_____

_____

_____

Questions for Discussion

Answer the following questions according to your perceptions to the best of your ability. Use an additional sheet of paper if necessary.

1. Do you feel that being Christians would make any difference in your sexual relationship?

2. Will you be able to discuss with your spouse what you do not know about sexual relations?

3. What worries you or preoccupies you concerning your sexual relationship?

4. After marriage, how do you expect to communicate your desire to have sexual intercourse?

5. Are there any memories of the past that would have a negative effect on your present attitude or feelings concerning your sexual relationship within marriage?

6. Can you recall the source from which you first heard about sexual reproduction? If so, explain.

7. Were you free to ask your parents questions about sex? What was their response?

8. Can you remember any specific attitudes or expressions of your parents concerning sexual relations?

9. Is it possible for marriage partners to be involved in lust towards one another?

10. Is there anything that embarrasses you concerning sexual relations?

11. How often do you expect to engage in sexual relations per month with your spouse?

12. Do you have any apprehension concerning sex within marriage? If so, explain.

13. What purpose, if any, would masturbation (self-stimulation) serve within a marriage?

14. What type(s) of contraceptives are you and your fiancé considering? Do you and your fiancé agree on birth control? Who will be responsible for birth control? Have you consulted your physician?

Attitudes and Beliefs about Sex

Place an *A* for agree or a *D* for disagree before each statement below.

_____ 1. It is not the woman's responsibility to initiate sexual relations.

_____ 2. Sexual response can diminish when tension exists in the marriage.

_____ 3. Sex should never be a scheduled activity.

_____ 4. Sexual intimacy is important to a rewarding marriage relationship.

_____ 5. Mutual orgasm always occurs with sexual intercourse.

_____ 6. Present sexual dysfunction may be the result of past sexual abuse or misinformation.

_____ 7. Sex should never be used as a reward or a punishment.

_____ 8. A couple should do all they can possibly do before considering counseling when experiencing sexual difficulties.

_____ 9. Abstaining from sexual intimacy is permissible when one partner is fasting.

_____ 10. It is permissible to withhold or demand sex from your spouse.

_____ 11. It is God's purpose for sex to be desirable and satisfying to both partners.

_____ 12. Making excuses in order to avoid sexual relations is natural and should be expected.

_____ 13. A married couple should fully communicate to each other what pleases them sexually.

_____ 14. Because your body is not your own, you or your spouse can request or be involved in any kind of sexual behavior within your marriage.

B.E.S.T.

In Dr. Ed Wheat's book *Love Life for Every Married Couple,* he presents a "prescription for a superb marriage." Couples need to put into practice all four measures of this prescription simultaneously and consistently. If you are not involved in blessing, edifying, sharing, and touching with your mate, you will begin to develop sexual disinterest. Take time to discuss these principles and how you will implement them in your marriage. Refer to this prescription regularly.

B   Blessing
E   Edifying
S   Sharing
T   Touching

1. **Blessing:** Four practical ways to bless (1 Peter 3:9–12)
   Loving words.
   Practical behavior (showing loving-kindness).
   Thankfulness (appreciation of one another).
   Intercessory prayer.
   Note: Your partner's bad behavior will not excuse yours.

2. **Edifying:** To build up one another's personality, increasing self-worth (Rom. 14:19; 15:2; 1 Thess. 5:11)
   Husband edifies wife by praising her.
   Wife edifies husband by her loving response.
   A wife's sense of her own beauty depends on what her husband says and thinks of her.
   The husband never criticizes in insecure, vulnerable areas.
   A wife's full-time job is to respect, admire, adore, esteem, praise, and deeply love her husband.
   A husband is dependent upon his wife's affirmations.
   Note: Never criticize. Admire positive qualities. Verbalize praise. Recognize privately and publicly.

3. **Sharing:** All areas of life (Heb. 13:6; 1 Tim. 6:18)

Share time, activities, interests, ideas, innermost thoughts, spiritual walk, family objectives, and goals.
Do things together.
Give of yourself, listen.
Be interested in other's interests.

4. **Touching:** Communicates caring

Touching needs to involve joyful, nonsexual touches—snuggling, sleeping close, sharing affection (building the love emotion for one another).
Set a date night.
Practice nonsexual "light touching."
Hold and caress.

Taken from *Love Life for Every Married Couple* by Ed Wheat, M.D. Copyright © 1980, 1987 by Ed Wheat, M.D. Used by permission of Zondervan Publishing House, Grand Rapids, Michigan.

A Creative Plan

Even though a creative plan cannot be implemented until after you say "I do," read and discuss these eight characteristics together with your premarital counselors. By being open and honest now, you can overcome inhibitions in becoming a creative lover.

I. Sexual Pleasure Is God's Idea
    A. Sexual pleasure is God's intent for marriage.
        1. Sex was God's idea. He gave it to us for our pleasure. Procreation is not the only purpose for sex.

    B. Sexual fulfillment is a process. It is a *learned* experience.
        1. Know God's intent. (Review the Sex in Marriage exercise, p. 51)
        2. God's desire is to encourage you and liberate you sexually.

    C. Open and honest communication about the sexual relationship is necessary.
        1. Clearly communicate what is enjoyable to you.
        2. Ask what is enjoyable to your spouse.

II. Eight Characteristics of a Creative Lover
    A. Be totally available—1 Corinthians 7:3–5
        1. Do not deprive your husband or wife except for prayer and fasting.
        2. Schedule nights for time together. Take a nap if necessary.
        3. If you find yourself lacking sexual desire, know that right action will generate desire.
        4. What is at stake when you say no? There is a possibility of damaging your spouse's self-esteem. *Note:* You can be a very loving wife or husband, but if you consistently turn your spouse down sexually, the other things you do will be negated.

    B. Be carefree.
        1. Know that sexual response for a woman is tied to her emotions.
        2. Put your cares aside and freely give yourself to one another.
        3. If there is a lot on your mind, pray, then give each other a backrub.
        4. If there is hurt between you, work it out before lovemaking.

C. Be attractive. Appearance affects our attraction to each other.
   1. Always do your best to be presentable/attractive to your spouse.
   2. Don't always look "grubby" at home.
   3. Take care of yourself (shower, shave, make-up, etc.) even if you aren't going out.
   4. Wear attractive underwear. Wear attractive nightwear. Use cologne and perfume.

D. Be eager. Anticipate sexual experiences with one another.
   1. Fantasize about one another.
   2. Let God liberate you to daydream about your physical time together (see Song of Solomon chapters 4 & 8).
   3. Practice thinking about your husband or wife. Think positive things about your physical relationship (see Phil. 4:8).

E. Be creative. Study your spouse. Find out what excites him or her. What turns him or her on? Pursue creative avenues to ignite these desires.
   1. Do things differently. Be romantic.
   2. Do not try to meet your spouse's need with what you like.
   3. Do not worry about other marriages. Study your own.

F. Be interested. Do not let lovemaking become predictable and boring.
   1. You do not serve the same frozen TV dinner every night, do you? Sex will lose its interest if you are not involved in doing things differently. Communicate about this.
   2. Are you willing to make love at unorthodox times? Are you willing to try new places? Are you willing to try new things?

G. Be uninhibited—Genesis 2:25
   1. Adam and Eve were naked and were not ashamed. They were totally free to give themselves without inhibitions.
   2. Accept yourself—your spouse chose *you!*
   3. Do not get hung up on imperfections.
   4. Do the things that you can do. Come to terms with how you look. Don't compare yourself.

5. Communicate with your spouse the area(s) you want to change (losing weight, gaining weight, cutting your hair, etc.).

H. Be aggressive. This advice is especially for the woman, because the man usually takes the initiative.
1. Totally give yourself—be excited, be thrilled.
2. Don't be boring and passive. Sexual relations are not just to meet biological needs.
3. Allow God to liberate you in responsiveness with consideration of your partner's feelings. Men should read 1 Peter 3:7.

III. In conclusion, be involved in these eight steps after marriage, and your sexual lives will blossom. Don't settle for second best. Decide to pursue God's desire of sexual pleasure in marriage.

IV. Points to Ponder:
A. Men are turned on by sight (e.g., undressing).
B. Women are turned on emotionally and by physical contact (e.g., light touching).
C. A woman is like an iron (she heats up slowly).
D. A man is like a light bulb (he turns on instantly).
E. Foreplay must be gentle and not rushed. Foreplay for the woman must begin before the bedroom.
F. Lovemaking takes time. There may be times when we meet biological needs only, but this is *not* the norm.
G. Use proper language.
H. Be clean, brush your teeth, shave, etc.

Ceremony Planning

This is your special day. What kind of wedding ceremony do you want to have? To help you begin, a sample ceremony is included on page 68. It is very important that you enjoy each aspect of the planning—from choosing invitations, gowns, and flowers to writing your vows and making arrangements for the honeymoon.

Your counselors will offer you helpful resources for planning your ceremony and writing your vows. This session also includes exercises addressing your call together and what's in a vow. On pages 65–67 you will find a study of what takes place in the spiritual realm during the wedding. Peruse these two pages carefully with your fiancé. Please direct any questions or comments that you may have to your counselors. You may also desire to cover some of these points with your parents.

Do not allow yourselves to become anxious or frustrated with details.

Bathe each decision in prayer. This is a one-time experience, and you will be grateful for happy memories.

Called Together?

Once again, congratulations are in order. You have completed five or more sessions in preparation for your life together. Hopefully, you now have a better understanding of the commitment you are about to make.

Perhaps you have come to the conclusion that you may not be ready for marriage. Even more painful than deciding not to get married at this point would be to spend your life feeling unsure if marriage was the right choice. If you have substantial reasons for not moving into marriage, do not ignore these convictions. Maturely and honestly acknowledge these reasons to your fiancé and counselor. Seek counsel and be absolutely sure about your decision.

However, we realize that many of you as a result of completing this study course, have increased in your desire to be married. Hopefully, you have been able to be honest and open, causing personal growth and enhancing your relationship.

Be sure to work for unity in deciding what kind of wedding ceremony *you* desire to have. This is your special day. Following are some questions to consider together when planning your wedding ceremony:

What do you want your wedding ceremony to reflect to the persons attending?_____

_____

Share several ways in which you would like to communicate God's presence in your ceremony. _____

_____

How do you want those who attend to participate in this celebration with you?_____

_____

Will you write your own vows?_____

_____

Do you want the officiating minister to deliver a sermon? If so, what message do you want him to share? _____

_____

Is your wedding budget reasonable? _____

_____

Have you discussed this budget with your parents? _____

_____

Are your parents helping financially with the wedding?_____

_____

Are there ways you should honor your parents in the ceremony? _____

_____

Have your parents expressed special preferences for the ceremony that you do not wish to include? _____

_____

If so, how will you deal with this? _____

_____

Finally, do not allow the excitement of this day to rob you of creating life-long memories. Most importantly, rejoice and be glad that two are being called together as one.

What's in a Vow?

"If a man makes a vow to the LORD, or swears an oath to bind himself by some agreement, he shall not break his word; he shall do according to all that proceeds out of his mouth" (Num. 30:2).

Webster defines *vow* as, "A solemn promise or pledge that commits one to act or behave in a particular way." That obligation, promise, or pledge would include your marriage vows. Marriage, according to Scripture, is a covenant to companionship. A covenant was the most binding contract in the Bible. It was an oath with great penalties if broken.

There should be no consideration given to the breaking of a marriage vow. The follower of Christ could not have disagreement enough for a divorce. Jesus said in Mark 10:9, "Therefore what God has joined together, let man not separate."

Your vows are spoken to one another, to God, and to those who witness your marriage ceremony. Do not take them lightly. Listen to what the book of Ecclesiastes states concerning a vow: "When you make a vow to God, do not delay to pay it: For He has no pleasure in fools. Pay what you have vowed—Better not to vow than to vow and not pay" (Eccles. 5:4–5).

What's in a vow? A commitment, a promise, a pledge, an obligation to remain married . . . "until death do us part."

Saying I Do: What Happens at a Wedding

The marriage union gives birth to many radical changes. The least visible of these changes take place in the spiritual realm. The following is a study outline intended to point out some of those important changes. Thoroughly cover the following with your fiancé and your premarital counselors.

I. A Transfer of Authority:
   A. Prior to the wedding the bride and the groom are under the authority of another.
      1. The woman comes to the wedding with her father (with whom she has spent most of her life) and leaves with her husband (with whom she will spend the remainder of her life).
      2. The man leaves father and mother to cleave to his wife.
   B. After the wedding, the husband is commanded to be the authority for another, his wife.
      1. This includes spiritual leadership, as well as the responsibility to care for and draw counsel from his wife.
   C. The woman changes her name.
      1. The father gives his daughter away.
      2. The bride accepts a new name.

II. An Exchange of Possessions:
   A. The husband and wife no longer belong to themselves. They will give of themselves in three areas:
      1. Their spirits—the most intimate area (where God dwells)
      2. Their souls—the intellect, will, and emotions
      3. Their bodies—the flesh (including the skills of the flesh)
   B. They give away their possessions:
      1. Automobiles, furniture, etc.
      2. Money
   C. They give away their problems:
      1. Physical
      2. Financial
      3. Relational

III. New Responsibility:
   A. ". . . the head of every man is Christ, the head of woman is man, and the head of Christ is God" (1 Cor. 11:3).
      1. A husband is responsible to Christ.
      2. A wife is responsible to her husband.
      3. Christ is responsible to God.
   B. As the husband is submitted to Christ, so the wife is responsible to be submitted to her husband, allowing him to be responsible for her.
   C. Husbands love your wives (Eph. 5:25–33; 1 Peter 3:7)
      1. Giving himself
      2. Honoring her, being considerate
      3. Giving of his name
      4. Caring for her
      5. Leaving past relationships
      6. Living for her (dying to himself)
      7. Treating her with respect

IV. New Purposes
   A. To give happiness (blessing) to another.
      1. Your happiness comes from making your spouse happy.
   B. To bring fulfillment to your spouse in marriage.
      1. Make your spouse's life meaningful.
   C. To experience the fullness of being complemented by another.

V. Schedule changes
   A. Major changes take place in individual schedules, environments, or even geographical areas.

VI. Additional Relationships
   A. Marriage into the spouse's family requires special love and grace.
   B. Accept and reach out to meet the needs of the in-laws.
   C. Involve yourself with the friends of your spouse and accept friendships you have brought into the marriage.
   D. Additional relationships will come after having children.

VII. Widen interests:
  A. As you receive the abilities, interests, and areas of expertise of your spouse, they become increasingly beneficial to you.
  B. As your spouse grows, rather than losing your identity, it becomes enriched by what your spouse adds to you.
  C. Interests should become mutually beneficial.
  D. Each mate is a lifetime study; you study your mate to know him/her and to understand his/her needs.
  E. Everything your mate is, knows, and is becoming is yours to share.

Adapted from the radio broadcast series, "What Happens at a Wedding," David Mains and Ted Place, October 10–15, 1989. Copyright © 1989 by The Chapel of the Air, Inc. Used by permission.

Sample Ceremony

The following marriage ceremony can help you begin planning your own special day. It includes the basic structure of a Christian wedding, as well as traditions found in many weddings. Ask the Holy Spirit to guide you as you creatively plan your marriage ceremony.

The Marriage Ceremony of
Mark Richard Windsor and Victoria Anne Chancery
February 14
2:00 PM

Prelude   (1:40 PM)

This Is the Day
Together As One
Make Us One
Great Is the Lord (Mark escorts in his parents as the pastor, Henry, Tom, and Jeff enter from the side door.)

Processional   (2:00 PM)

Joyful, Joyful	(Bridesmaids enter)
Bridal Chorus	(Victoria and her father enter)

Giving of the Bride   Pastor

Pastor: "Who gives this bride in marriage?"
Father: "Her mother and I."
(Mark steps forward. Mark and Victoria face the front.)

Prayer   Pastor

"I ask that the congregation remain standing as we come before the Lord in prayer."

"The congregation may be seated."

Message (10–15 minutes)   Pastor

(Include charge of faith to couple and witnesses.)

"Wives, submit to your own husbands, as to the Lord. For the husband is head of the wife, as also Christ is head of the church; and He is the Savior of the body.

Therefore, just as the church is subject to Christ, so let the wives be to their own husbands in everything. Husbands, love your wives, just as Christ also loved the church and gave Himself for her, that He might sanctify and cleanse her with the washing of water by the word, that He might present to Himself a glorious church, not having spot or wrinkle or any such thing, but that she should be holy and without blemish. So husbands ought to love their wives as their own bodies; he who loves his wife loves himself. For no one ever hated his own flesh, but nourishes and cherishes it, just as the Lord does the church. For we are members of His body, of His flesh and of His bones. 'For this reason a man shall leave his father and mother and be joined to his wife, and the two shall become one flesh.' This is a great mystery, but I speak concerning Christ and the church." (Eph. 5:22–32)

To Groom: "Have you received Jesus Christ as Lord and Savior of your life?"
Response: "I have."

To Bride: "Have you received Jesus Christ as Lord and Savior of your life?"
Response: "I have."

"The Bible tells us that any man who is in Christ is a new creation; old things have passed away and all things have become new. Mark and Victoria, your expression of faith makes you one with Jesus Christ!"

To You As Witnesses

"To the congregation, as well as to the world, I announce that Mark and Victoria stand before you cleansed by the shed blood of their personal Savior, Jesus.

"Jesus said in the eighteenth chapter of Matthew's gospel, *'Again, I say unto you, that if two of you agree on earth concerning anything that they will ask, it will be done for them of My Father in heaven.'*

"You as a congregation are here to bear witness of this marriage. You are also here to stand before God in agreement with this union. Mark and Victoria desire your blessing upon their call together."

(Mark & Victoria move up onto platform.)

Profession of Vows   Pastor

To Groom: "Mark, do you take Victoria to be your wife, to be one with your flesh, to love her as Christ loves the church, to be faithful to her the remainder of your life?"

Response: "I do."

To Groom: "Please turn to Victoria and make this profession of your faith to her."

(Hand card to Mark. He reads it.)

Groom: "I, Mark, take you, Victoria, to be my wife. I promise before God and these witnesses to be your loving and faithful husband, in plenty and in want, in joy and in sorrow, in adversity and in health, as long as we both shall live."

To Bride: "Victoria, do you take Mark to be your husband, to be one with his flesh, submitting yourself to him as unto the Lord, showing reverence to him as the head of this union for the remainder of your life?"

Response: "I do."

To Bride: "Please turn to Mark and make this profession of your faith."

(Hand card to Victoria. She reads it.)

Bride: "I, Victoria, take you, Mark, to be my husband. I promise before God and these witnesses to be your loving and faithful wife, in plenty and in want, in joy and in sorrow, in adversity and in health, as long as we both shall live."

Presentation of the Rings   Pastor

(Get rings from best man)

"May I have the rings please? This ring is a cherished symbol—an outward expression of your faith and a token of your love to one another. This ring is made of gold, a precious metal. It is a perfect, never-ending circle that symbolizes the continuing love of God and the gift of eternal life. These rings serve as a reminder of God's love for you, your love for one another, and the commitment you are making to one another today."

(Give Victoria's ring to Mark)

To Groom: "Mark, take this ring, place it on Victoria's finger, and as you do, repeat this confession of faith to her:

"With this ring, I thee wed. I give it as a token of my faith and my love, in the name of Jesus."
(Give Mark's ring to Victoria)

To Bride: "Victoria, take this ring, place it on Mark's finger, and as you do, repeat this confession of faith to him:
"With this ring, I thee wed. I give it as a token of my faith and my love, in the name of Jesus."

Pronouncement   Pastor

"Join right hands please. (Pastor puts hand on Mark's and Victoria's hands) By the authority vested in me as a representative of Jesus Christ and as a minister of His gospel, and in the name of the Father, of His Son Jesus, and by the power of the Holy Spirit of God, I now pronounce you united together as husband and wife. What God has joined together, let no man put asunder! You may kiss the bride!"

(Music begins immediately after the kiss)

Lighting of the Unity Candle   (While song *Author of Love* plays)

Communion   (Pastor explains)

"Mark and Victoria believe that it is appropriate to seal their marriage by sharing communion together. Mark and Victoria serve a living God. Jesus Christ, who has risen from the dead, gives us resurrection power. As you eat this bread and drink this cup, you are again receiving by faith the resurrection power of Jesus Christ to be the husband and wife that God has called you to be."

(Give the bread and juice)

Song   (*Our Desire*)

Prayer and Blessing   Pastor

"Now may the God of patience and comfort grant you to be like-minded toward one another, according to Christ Jesus, that you may with one mind

and one mouth glorify the God and Father of our Lord Jesus Christ.
"Therefore receive one another, just as Christ also received us, to the glory of God." (Rom. 15:5–7)

(Mark and Victoria turn and face the congregation)

Presentation of the Bride and Groom   Pastor
"Ladies and gentlemen, I present to you Mr. and Mrs. Mark Windsor!"

Recessional   *(Hallelujah Chorus)*
Mark and Victoria exit. Bridal party follows. Ushers come forward.

Pastor signs marriage license and returns vow cards.

Honeymoon Expectations

The honeymoon is a special time. Everyday life is set aside so the two of you are free to enjoy each other. It is important to keep in mind that your focus is not the things you will be doing, but on the time you will spend together making memories. It should be a time so significant that you will enjoy reminiscing about it for the rest of your lives.

This is where expectations come in. Do you expect the honeymoon to be perfect? Will it be without a disagreement or quarrel? Will it be one hundred percent romantic? Of course, neither one of you could become sick . . .

Here are some questions for you to respond to concerning the honeymoon:

1. Why am I looking forward to our honeymoon? _____

_____

_____

2. What are my apprehensions concerning our honeymoon? _____

_____

_____

3. What if the weather does not cooperate? _____

_____

_____

4. What if our travel plans go awry? _____

_____

_____

5. What if the menstrual period occurs during our honeymoon? _____

_____

_____

6. Are we in agreement with what we are doing, where we are going, and how long a honeymoon we are taking?_____

_____

_____

7. Have you scheduled your wedding ceremony early enough in the day so that your wedding night does not begin too late? _____

_____

_____

8. When will we schedule our second honeymoon? _____

_____

_____

Probably the sexual relationship comes to mind most often when a young couple thinks of their honeymoon. Expectations in this area can lead to much disappointment or unexpected satisfaction. Please keep in mind that learning to respond to each other sexually is a life-long process. What you experience on your wedding night and throughout your honeymoon should be unique to you as a couple.

After your honeymoon, be prepared to step back into everyday life with jobs, schedules, and demands being placed upon you. Your honeymoon needs to serve as the foundation for maintaining romance and closeness throughout your Christ-centered marriage. And remember, when you do have disagreements, it will be your opportunity to put into practice what you have learned throughout the premarital program and to experience the beauty of forgiveness and healing.

After
the
Ceremony

Postmarital training is almost unheard of. But why shouldn't we have it? The first year of marriage is foundational. There are so many adjustments to make, so many questions that arise. If the premarital instruction was helpful to you, think about how effective the reinforcement of those principles could be, along with accountability to a Christian couple, after you've said, "I do."

God encourages one full year of foundation building. His Word states in Deuteronomy 24:5, "When a man has taken a new wife, he shall not go out to war or be charged with any business; he shall be free at home one year, and bring happiness to his wife whom he has taken."

This course can be studied by those newly married or by those who have been married for some time and would like to evaluate their relationship.

Congratulations!

Congratulations are in order again now that you have become one in Jesus Christ.

This postmarital course is designed to help you build a firm foundation for your marriage. Please complete the following exercises before postmarital session number one (Three Months) and session number two (Nine Months). Take your assignments seriously and please be honest. If there are areas of conflict within your marriage there will be no better time than now to pray and work through them.

If personality profiles were used in your premarital counseling, bring them along with your *Called Together* manuals to postmarital session number one. Do not hesitate to ask any question of your postmarital counselors. They are ready and willing to serve you.

"Have you not read . . . 'For this reason a man shall leave his father and mother and be joined to his wife, and the two shall become one flesh'? So then they are no longer two but one. Therefore what God has joined together, let man not separate" (Matt. 19:5–6).

God bless you, as you've been *Called Together!*

Three Months

Ninety days have come and gone since you spoke that sacred marriage vow to one another. Hopefully it has been the best ninety days of your life. Ninety days seems to be a key term in our society. We hear, for example, the following: "Full refund within ninety days if not completely satisfied"; "No interest for ninety days"; "Ninety days same as cash." What is being communicated is that in ninety days, reality begins to set in.

You have a lifetime to fulfill your commitment to your partner. The honeymoon does not need to come to an end after ninety days. You will begin to learn that romance is a vital element in keeping a marriage relationship fresh and exciting. Don't let your relationship grow stale. Ask the Holy Spirit to remind you of creative ways to express your love: remembering special occasions; giving flowers, cards, and candy; writing love notes; etc. Be innovative with your partner. The "reality" is that marriage is a day-to-day commitment.

The first exercise is designed to provoke you into a more knowledgeable communication pattern, while the second exercise provides the opportunity to write about emotional needs. Scenario Response, the third exercise, will cause you to think about situations in which married couples often find themselves. You will explore ways to be "wise builders" in Firm Foundation, and in Discovering the Differences you will give thought to possible personal differences. One of the final exercises will give you the unique opportunity to rate your spouse. The last two exercises will provide many ideas for ways to show love to your spouse. Be honest with all of your responses and have a great time.

Expanding Our Communication Knowledge

Read and study this exercise together.

James talks about two kinds of wisdom. He says: "Who is wise and understanding among you? Let him show by good conduct that his works are done in the meekness of wisdom. But if you have bitter envy and self-seeking in your hearts, do not boast and lie against the truth. This wisdom does not descend from above, but is earthly, sensual, demonic" (3:13–16).

Earthly "wisdom" causes conflict. Envy and selfish ambition give birth to disorder and evil practices. Envying your sister in the Lord because her husband is "more spiritual" than your husband reveals selfish ambition and produces conflict.

"But the wisdom that is from above is first pure, then peaceable, gentle, willing to yield, full of mercy and good fruits, without partiality and without hypocrisy. Now the fruit of righteousness is sown in peace by those who make peace" (James 3:17–18).

Heavenly wisdom gives birth to divine order and righteous practices. "Surely He scorns the scornful, but gives grace to the humble" (Prov. 3:34). When you respond to your mate with heavenly wisdom (consideration, submission, love, mercy, etc.), envy and selfish ambition must flee: "Therefore submit to God. Resist the devil and he will flee from you" (James 4:7). Furthermore, if you sow peace you will reap a harvest of peace.

James 4:1 raises the question, "What causes fights and quarrels among you?" James's answer is, "Don't they come from your desires that battle within you? You want something but don't get it. You kill and covet, but you cannot have what you want. You quarrel and fight. You do not have, because you do not ask God" (NIV).

Herein lies the answer to why we have conflict; we want something but we are not getting it. Think about any conflict, past or present. You expressed a desire for something. You did not receive it or you were given something in the place of it. Hurt and/or anger arose within you. You were wronged, taken advantage of, not listened to, or ignored.

Perhaps as a child you wanted a specific kind and color of bicycle for Christmas. What happened when you didn't get what you wanted? Suppose you ask your husband to wash the dishes while you attend a meeting. He forgets, and you have to do them the next morning before work. Suppose you ask your wife to iron your favorite shirt for an important meeting. She gets involved in a lengthy telephone conversation, and you are forced to iron the shirt yourself.

What is important now is your response. Will you become selfish and demanding, even accusing?

You may be tempted to use "you" statements, such as "You're always on the phone." "Can't you ever cook a decent breakfast?" "You're always trying to make me into something I'm not." "You never clean the house." You may also be tempted to use "I told you so" statements: "You continually have to have it your way." "Well, I hope you're satisfied." "Maybe someday you'll learn to take my advice." If you become demanding you will be placing condemnation upon your spouse. Condemnation rarely motivates anyone to do anything. Instead, it makes people feel defensive. Your spouse will interpret your behavior as critical and insensitive and will want to accuse you in return.

These negative "you" statements must be replaced. Avoid using "you" statements when sharing how you feel. Wait until your anger has subsided, then replace "you" statements with "I feel" messages. Let's use two of the "you" statement examples to illustrate this point:

"you" statement	"I feel" message
"You're always on the phone."	"Honey, you probably didn't realize it, but I felt like you didn't care about whether my shirt was ironed or not."

"you" statement	"I feel" message
"You're always trying to make me into something I'm not."	"I realize that I'm not perfect and that I have a long way to go, but I really don't understand all the ways that I offend you. I feel like I'm not being accepted for who I am. Can we discuss it?"

When demanding our way, we often use words that tear down rather than edify. Resist that selfish desire and submit your communication to God. As husband and wife, you need to hold one another accountable for how you make each other feel. You must have the courage to reveal how you feel through a soft "answer" in order to avoid criticizing and creating defensive attitudes.

"Anyone, then, who knows the good he ought to do and doesn't do it, sins" (James 4:17).

List some of the "you" statements that you may have spoken to your spouse and turn them into "I feel" messages.

"you" statement   **"I feel" message**

_____   _____

_____   _____

_____   _____

_____   _____

_____   _____

"you" statement   **"I feel" message**

_____   _____

_____   _____

_____   _____

_____   _____

_____   _____

Emotional Needs

Complete the following without the input of your spouse.

A. List ten of your personal emotional needs.
   (Examples of emotional needs include appreciation, affection, respect.)

1. _____

2. _____

3. _____

4. _____

5. _____

6. _____

7. _____

8. _____

9. _____

10. _____

B. List ten of your spouse's personal emotional needs.

1. _____

2. _____

3. _____

4. _____

5. _____

6. _____

7. _____

8. _____

9. _____

10. _____

C. Do you feel as though your spouse misinterprets your emotional needs? If yes, explain:

_____

_____

_____

_____

_____

_____

_____

Scenario Response

Complete this exercise individually.

1. How is the "ideal" marriage different from your marriage?

2. Because of a greater familiarity with your spouse, you now feel tempted to say things or do things you would not have considered saying or doing during your engagement. How will you handle this temptation?

Imagine the following scenarios:

3. You have taken the time to communicate some important information with your spouse. Your spouse did not hear you the first time, so you are now repeating your statement. In the middle of repeating this information a second time, your spouse says rather bluntly, "Would you stop mumbling and speak up so I can hear you?" What is your response?

4. You and your spouse have agreed to spend $50 per week on groceries. Your partner returns home from grocery shopping ecstatic about "all the great deals." You ask, "How much did you spend?" His/her response is, "$65." What is your response?

5. You have communicated a desire for sexual relations. Your spouse also seems to agree excitedly. In the middle of your evening prayer time, your spouse falls asleep. This would be OK except that this is the third night in a row that this has happened. What is your response?

Firm Foundation

Please complete this exercise with your spouse.

Read Matthew 7:24–27. Jesus describes the wise and the foolish builders in the text. Please describe the areas in which the two of you see yourselves building upon a firm foundation for marriage.

1. _____

_____

_____

_____

2. _____

_____

_____

_____

3. _____

_____

_____

_____

4. _____

_____

_____

_____

5. _____

_____

_____

_____

Discovering the Differences

Complete this exercise without the help of your spouse.

1. Have you discovered any likes or dislikes on the part of your spouse that you were not aware of before marriage? Please elaborate.

Remember that Paul wrote in 2 Corinthians 5:17 that we are becoming a new creation.

2. Are your mate's moral and spiritual values what you thought they were before you were married?

Jesus said in Matthew 6:21 that where our treasure is our heart will be also.

3. Have you discovered any behavioral changes, positive or negative, in yourself or your spouse since marriage?

Romans 15:7 says to accept one another. James 1:22–23 admonishes us to be doers of the Word.

4. Have you discovered any habits (good or not so good) that you were not aware of before marriage? Please elaborate.

1 Thessalonians 5:15 admonishes us to make sure that nobody pays back wrong for wrong, but to be kind to each other.

5. Have you discovered any problems from your past that are now manifesting themselves in your marriage?

Galatians 5:1 tells us that Christ set us free for freedom's sake. God also states in Micah 7:18–19 that He delights in mercy and compassion. Ephesians 4:17–25 encourages us to put off the old and put on the new.

Rate Your Spouse

Below you are given the opportunity to evaluate your spouse. Be honest in your evaluation and remember that these are just your perceptions.

	Needs to Improve	Improving	Good	Very Good
1. Decision making				
2. Conflict resolution				
3. Finances				
4. Jealousy				
5. Hobbies (time balanced)				
6. Moodiness				
7. Temper				
8. Dependability				
9. Job (responsibility)				
10. Recreation (time balanced)				
11. Television (time balanced)				
12. Telephone				
13. Affection				
14. Friendships				
15. Praying together				
16. Spending time with you				
17. Relatives (relationships)				
18. Sense of humor				
19. Time with God				
20. Communication				

Ways a Husband May Express Love to His Wife

How to Convince Your Wife You Love Her

Evaluate the way you express love to your wife. Go over this list and circle any ways you may be neglecting to show love for your wife. Ask your wife to go over the list and put a check mark in front of the ways she would like you to express love. Ask her to add other things to the list.

1. Function as the loving leader of your home.
2. Frequently tell her you love her.
3. If she does not work outside the home, give her an agreed upon amount of money to spend in any way she chooses.
4. Lead family devotions regularly.
5. Smile and be cheerful when you come home from work.
6. Share the household chores.
7. Take care of the children for at least three hours every week so that she has free time to do whatever she wants.
8. Take her out for dinner or to do some fun thing at least once a week.
9. Do the "fix-it" jobs she wants done around the house.
10. Greet her when you come home with a smile, a hug, a kiss, and an "Am I glad to see you. I really missed you today."
11. Give her a lingering kiss.
12. Pat her on the shoulder, hold her hand, caress her frequently.
13. Be willing to talk to her about her concerns and not belittle her for having those.
14. Look at her with an adoring expression.
15. Sit close to her.
16. Rub her back.
17. Shave or take a bath or brush your teeth before you have sexual relations.
18. Wear her favorite after-shave lotion.
19. Write love notes or letters to her.
20. Let her know you appreciate her and what you appreciate about her. Do this often and for things that are sometimes taken for granted.

21. Fulfill her implied or unspoken wishes as well as the specific requests she makes of you.
22. Anticipate what she might like and surprise her by doing it before she asks.
23. Play with her; share her hobbies and recreational preferences enthusiastically; include her in yours.
24. Set a good example before the children.
25. Talk about her favorably to the children when she can hear you, and even when she cannot.
26. Brag about her good points to others; let her know you are proud to have her as your wife.
27. Maintain your own spiritual life through Bible study, prayer, regular church attendance, and fellowship with God's people.
28. Structure your time and use it wisely; be on time to go places.
29. Make plans prayerfully and carefully.
30. Ask her advice when you have problems or decisions to make.
31. Follow her advice unless to do so would violate biblical principles.
32. Fulfill your responsibilities.
33. Be sober, but not somber, about life.
34. Have a realistic, biblical, positive attitude toward life.
35. Discuss plans with your wife before you make decisions, and when the plans are made, share them fully with your wife, giving reasons for making the decisions you did.
36. Thank her in creative ways for her attempts to please you.
37. Ask forgiveness often, and say, "I was wrong and will try to change."
38. Actually change where and when you should.
39. Share your insights and good experiences with her.
40. Plan a mini-honeymoon.
41. Give some expression of admiration when she wears a new dress or your favorite negligee.
42. Gently brush her leg under the table.
43. Be reasonably happy to go shopping with her.
44. Relate what happened at work or whatever you did apart from her.
45. Reminisce about the early days of your marriage.
46. Express appreciation for her parents and relatives.
47. Take her out to breakfast.

48. Agree with her about getting a new dress or some other item.
49. Thank her when she supports your decisions and cooperates enthusiastically. Especially make it a matter of celebration when she supports and helps enthusiastically at times when you know she doesn't fully agree.
50. Ask her to have sexual relations with you and seek to be especially solicitous of her desires. Express gratitude when she tries to please you.
51. Buy gifts for her.
52. Remember anniversaries and other events that are special to her.
53. Watch the TV program she wants to watch or go where she wants to go instead of doing what you want to do. Do it cheerfully and enthusiastically.
54. Be cooperative and appreciative when she holds you, caresses or kisses you.
55. Be cooperative when she tries to arouse you and desires to have sexual relations. Never make fun of her for expressing her desires.
56. Run errands gladly.
57. Pamper her and make a fuss over her.
58. Be willing to see things from her point of view.
59. Be lovingly honest with her—no withholding of the truth that may hinder your present or future relationship.
60. Indicate you want to be alone with her and talk or just lie in each other's arms.
61. Refuse to "cop out," "blow up," attack, shift blame, withdraw, or exaggerate when she seeks to make constructive suggestions or discuss problems.
62. Give her your undivided attention when she wants to talk.
63. Cheerfully stay up past your bedtime to solve problems or share her burdens.
64. Get up in the middle of the night to take care of the children so that she may continue to sleep.
65. Hold her close while expressing tangible and vocal love when she is hurt, discouraged, weary, or burdened.
66. Plan vacations and trips with her.
67. Help her yourself instead of telling the children to "help Mommy."
68. Be eager to share a good joke or some other interesting information you have learned.

69. Join with her in a team ministry in the church.
70. Do a Bible study or research project together.
71. Establish a family budget.
72. Keep yourself attractive and clean.
73. Be a cooperative, helpful host when you have people over for dinner or fellowship.
74. Ask her to pray with you about something.
75. Spend time with the children in play, study, and communication.
76. Acknowledge that there are some specific areas or ways in which you need to improve.
77. Refuse to disagree with her in the presence of others.
78. Cooperate with her in establishing family goals and then in fulfilling them.
79. Be available and eager to fulfill her desires whenever and wherever possible and proper.
80. Begin each day with cheerfulness and tangible expressions of affection.
81. Plan to spend some time alone with her for sharing and communicating every day.
82. Remember to tell her when you must work late.
83. Refuse to work late on a regular basis.
84. Take care of the yard work properly.
85. Help the children with their homework.
86. Refuse to compare her unfavorably with other people.
87. Handle money wisely.
88. Don't allow work, church, or recreational activities to keep you from fulfilling marriage or family responsibilities.
89. Try to find things to do with her.
90. Be willing to go out or stay home with her.
91. Be polite to her.
92. Refuse to be overly dependent on your parents or friends.
93. Develop mutual friends.
94. Provide adequate hospitalization insurance.
95. Make provision for housing and some support for your family in case you should die or become handicapped.
96. Be especially helpful when she is not feeling well.
97. Be on time.

98. Go to P.T.A. meetings with her.

99. Let her sleep in once in a while by feeding the children breakfast and, if possible, getting them off to school.

100. Frequently give in to her and allow her to have her own way unless to do so would be sinful.

101. Put the children to bed at night.

102. Be gentle and tender and hold her before and after sexual relations.

103. Don't nit-pick and find fault; and don't give the impression that you expect her to be perfect.

Adapted from *A Homework Manual for Biblical Counseling, Volume 2* by Wayne Mack. Copyright © 1980. Used by permission of Presbyterian and Reformed Publishing Company, Phillipsburg, New Jersey.

Ways a Wife May Express Love to Her Husband

How to Convince Your Husband You Love Him

Evaluate the way you express love to your husband. Go over the list and circle the ways you are neglecting. Ask your husband to go over the list and put a check mark in front of the ways he would like you to express love. Ask him to add other things to the list.

1. Greet him at the door when he comes home with a smile, a hug, a kiss, and an "Am I glad to see you. I really missed you today."
2. Have a cup of coffee or tea ready for him when he comes home from work or a trip.
3. Give him a lingering kiss.
4. Let him know you like to be with him and make arrangements so that you can spend time with him without giving the impression that you really should or would rather be doing something else.
5. Be willing to talk to him about his concerns without belittling him for having these concerns.
6. Support him and cooperate with him enthusiastically when he has made a decision.
7. Tease and flirt with him.
8. Seek to arouse him and sometimes be the aggressor in sexual relations.
9. Ask him to have sexual relations more than he would expect you to.
10. Express yourself passionately during sexual relations.
11. Caress him.
12. Look at him with an adoring expression.
13. Sit close to him.
14. Hold his hand.
15. Rub his back.
16. Wear his favorite nightgown or dress or perfume.
17. Express your love in words or notes.
18. Let him know how much you appreciate him and what you appreciate about him. Do this often and for things that are sometimes taken for granted.

19. Frequently fulfill his unspoken wishes as well as the specific requests he makes of you. Try to anticipate what he might like and surprise him by doing it before he asks.

20. Play with him (tennis, golf, party games, etc.).

21. Enthusiastically share with him in devotions and prayer; seek to set a good example for the children concerning their attitude toward devotions and prayer.

22. Maintain your own spiritual life through regular Bible study and prayer.

23. Structure your time and use it wisely.

24. Be willing to face and solve problems even if it requires discomfort, change, and much effort.

25. Fulfill your responsibilities.

26. Ask him for his advice and frequently follow it.

27. Be ready to leave at the appointed time.

28. Stand with him and support him in his attempts to raise your children for God.

29. Thank him in creative ways for his attempts to please you.

30. Ask for forgiveness; say, "I was wrong and will try to change."

31. Actually change areas of your life that you know need changing.

32. Work with him on his projects.

33. Read books or magazine articles he asks you to read and share your insights.

34. Let him know when he has to make decisions that you really believe he will choose the right thing and that you will wholeheartedly support him in whatever decision he makes, provided the decision does not violate clearly revealed biblical principles. Be his best cheerleader and fan.

35. Buy gifts for him.

36. Show genuine interest in his hobbies: watch or attend sporting events with him; listen to him sing and play the guitar or piano; attend a class he teaches.

37. Find a mutually agreeable way to keep the house neat and clean.

38. Cook creative and nutritious meals—or praise him when he does.

39. Have devotions with the children when he is not able to be there.

40. Maintain his disciplinary rules when he is not present.

41. Be appreciative and responsive when he holds you, caresses or kisses you.
42. Lovingly give him your input when you think he is in error.
43. Offer constructive suggestions when you think he could improve or become more productive. Don't push or preach or do this in such a way that you belittle him, but seek positive and nonthreatening ways to help him become more fully the man God wants him to be.
44. Run errands gladly.
45. Seek to complete, not compete with, him; be the best member on his team and seek to convince him that you are just that.
46. Be lovingly honest with him—no withholding of truth that will hinder your relationship or future trust and closeness.
47. Be willing to see things from his point of view; believe the best about what he does or says.
48. Pamper him and make a fuss over him.
49. Be happy and cheerful.
50. Refuse to nag.
51. Gently brush his leg under the table.
52. Have candlelight and music at dinner.
53. Indicate you want to be alone with him to talk or just lie in his arms.
54. Give a "suggestive" wink.
55. Go for a walk with him.
56. Let him know you feel lonely when he is out of town.
57. Tell him what happened to you during your day.
58. Share your fears, concerns, joys, failures, etc.
59. Seek to support your ideas with biblical insights and practical wisdom.
60. Refuse to "cop out," withdraw, attack, exaggerate, or shift blame when he seeks to make constructive suggestions or discuss problems.
61. Give him your undivided attention when he wants to talk.
62. Discuss the meaning of certain Bible passages or discuss how to improve your marriage, home, children, or child-raising efforts.
63. Cheerfully stay up past your bedtime to resolve a disagreement or problem.
64. Hold him close and express genuine concern with tangible and vocal love when he is hurt, discouraged, weary, or burdened.

65. Be eager to share a good joke or some other interesting information you have learned.
66. Work in the yard, paint a room together, or wash the car.
67. Plan vacations or trips together.
68. Keep your family memorabilia, newspaper clippings, church bulletins, etc.
69. Brag to others about his accomplishments and tell them what a good husband he is.
70. Join with him in a team ministry at the church.
71. Do a Bible study or Bible research project together.
72. Keep up with family finances.
73. Help prepare the income tax report.
74. Keep in touch with your family and friends through letters.
75. Keep yourself attractive and clean.
76. Invite his friends or work associates over for dinner or fellowship.
77. Develop and use the spiritual gifts God has given you.
78. Ask him to pray with you.
79. Express how much you love the children and be their cheerleader.
80. Stay within the family budget; save some money for special surprises.
81. Be excited about sharing the gospel, celebrating answered prayer, or helping other people.
82. Make a list of things that need to be done around the house.
83. Be satisfied with your present standard of living, furniture, and appliances when you cannot afford to upgrade them.
84. Don't make nostalgic comments about your father that might imply that you think your father is a much better man than your husband.
85. Acknowledge that there are some specific areas in which you need to improve.
86. Appreciate and help his family.
87. Refuse to disagree with him in the presence of others.
88. Cooperate with him in establishing family goals.
89. Be unconventional in your lovemaking.
90. Tell him before he asks that you think he has done a good job. Don't be afraid of repeating yourself in commending him for what he is or does.

91. Be available and eager to fulfill his desires wherever and whenever it is proper and possible.
92. Begin each day with cheerfulness and tangible expressions of affection.
93. Let the children know that you and your husband agree; communicate to your children when your husband can hear (and when he cannot) how wonderful he is.

Adapted from *A Homework Manual for Biblical Counseling, Volume 2* by Wayne Mack. Copyright © 1980. Used by permission of Presbyterian and Reformed Publishing Company, Phillipsburg, New Jersey.

Nine Months

Postmarital Session Two

Your first anniversary is just three months away! You have been married almost a year! How are you feeling about your marriage, your spouse, and the foundation you have been building for the past nine months? Are you meeting the goals you established for your first year of marriage? Are you feeling disillusioned in any areas of your marriage relationship?

This nine-month checkup was designed to assist you as a couple to reevaluate your goals, priorities, finances, communication patterns, and sexual relationship. Challenge yourselves to pursue a new level of commitment in your marriage relationship as you proceed through the following exercises.

The first exercise, Opposite Relations, focuses on your strengths and weaknesses as a couple, while the second exercise provides a candid approach to discussing various areas of marriage. The next exercise centers on sexual relations, while the exercise titled Goals provides an opportunity to consider your goals together. Rate your spouse in the following exercise and then re-work your annual budget. The postmarital study concludes with a discussion of the three parts of human beings and with one of the most important topics of marriage: forgiveness. Enjoy yourselves.

Opposite Relationships

Complete this exercise as a couple.

A. Discuss the ways in which you are opposites. How can these differences strengthen your relationship? Discuss how the enemy (Satan) would like to use these differences to weaken your relationship.

B. What gifts does your spouse have that you do not have?

C. Discuss several incidents that have drawn you closer to your spouse.

D. How you can tell when your spouse is unhappy with you?

E. Which one of you is more task oriented? Which one of you is more relational? Discuss how this can be a strength, as well as a weakness.

For Further Discussion

Complete the following without the help of your spouse.

1. In what ways are you still tied to your parents?

2. Do you as a couple have other couples as close friends?

3. Do you as an individual still maintain close, same-sex friendships? Do you have a "best" friend?

4. Do you enjoy your job? Does your spouse support you working where you do? Do you have a tendency to bring work frustrations home with you?

5. In what ways do you feel your spouse is dependent upon you?

6. Is there something that you do not understand about your spouse?

7. In what ways are you secure in your spouse's commitment?

8. (a) How have you attempted to change your spouse?

(b) How has your spouse attempted to change you?

9. Does your spouse consider your feelings before making a decision?

10. Are there any ways in which you feel as though you have failed to meet your spouse's needs?

11. Please list your first five priorities (for example: job, spouse, God, mother, children, ministry).

12. Are there any activities in your spouse's life that you feel are more important than you are?

13. When you have exposed your weaknesses, how has your spouse made you feel?

14. Have you hurt or offended your spouse in any way?

15. Is your spouse willing to admit that he/she is wrong?

16. Is your spouse willing to apologize?

17. Can your spouse accept advice/counsel from you? From others?

18. Does your spouse have any negative habits or attitudes that have affected your marriage?

19. Is your spouse still tied to his/her parents?

20. How much time do you as an individual and as a couple spend watching television?

    What effect does television have on your marriage relationship?
    _____strong effect   _____average effect   _____little effect

    Please elaborate.

Sexual Communication Exercise

Complete the following without the input of your spouse. Please be honest in your answers. Mark your answers by making a check in the yes (most of the time), no (seldom), or sometimes column.

	Yes	No	Sometimes
1. Do you enjoy your sexual relationship?			
2. Do you feel that your partner enjoys your sexual relationship?			
3. Do you and your partner agree on the frequency of sexual intercourse?			
4. Do you understand your partner's sexual needs and desires?			
5. Does your partner understand your sexual needs and desires?			
6. Do you make your sexual needs known to your partner?			
7. Does your partner make his/her sexual needs known to you?			
8. Do you and your partner take sufficient time to engage in foreplay?			
9. Do you avoid discussing any sexual areas or needs?			
10. Do you feel your partner avoids discussing any sexual areas?			
11. Have you discussed sexual problems with anyone other than your spouse?			
12. Is it difficult for you to ask your partner to engage in sex?			

	Yes	No	Sometimes
13. Do you and your partner pray about your sexual relationship?			
14. Have you and your partner studied any books on the sexual union?			
15. Is your partner affectionate with you outside of sexual intercourse?			
16. Are you affectionate with your partner outside of sexual intercourse?			
17. Do you and your partner discuss problems within your sexual relationship?			
18. Have you ever refused to fulfill your partner's sexual request?			
19. Has your partner ever refused to fulfill a sexual request from you?			
20. Are you able to share with your partner what you find enjoyable sexually?			
21. Does your partner share with you what he/she finds enjoyable sexually?			

Complete these statements.

22. Our sex life has been _____

_____

23. Sexually I wish _____

_____

24. In the future I hope our sex life will _____

_____

Goals

You may feel that it is too soon to begin looking at life goals. But as the saying goes, "If you aim for nothing, you'll always hit it." Goals are important. Norm Wright states in his book *Training Christians to Counsel* that in order to create a good goal," . . . it must have three characteristics: (1) it must be specific (well-defined, to the point); (2) it must be realistic, or attainable; (3) it must have a time limit (next week, this summer, in twenty years—someday does not count)."

List, as a couple, several goals in the areas indicated. Please remember to be specific and realistic and to set a time limit.

A. Spiritual goals (example: a mission team trip, individual devotional time)

B. Physical goals (example: to lose weight, to be more sexually responsive)

C. Financial goals (example: to save $50 per paycheck, to purchase a house)

D. Family goals (example: when to start our family, number of children)

E. Employment goals (example: to be branch manager)

Rate Your Spouse

Below you are given the opportunity to evaluate your spouse. Be honest in your evaluation and remember that these are just your perceptions.

	Needs to Improve	Improving	Good	Very Good
1. Decision making				
2. Conflict resolution				
3. Finances				
4. Jealousy				
5. Hobbies (time balanced)				
6. Moodiness				
7. Temper				
8. Dependability				
9. Job (responsibility)				
10. Recreation (time balanced)				
11. Television (time balanced)				
12. Telephone				
13. Affection				
14. Friendships				
15. Praying together				
16. Spending time with you				
17. Relatives (relationships)				
18. Sense of humor				
19. Time with God				
20. Communication				

Personal Finances Budget Sheet

Since two incomes merge into one after marriage, it is important to once again go over the financial budget sheet. As a couple, you should now have a better picture of your financial needs and goals.

You will need to locate an appropriate time and place in order to begin re-working your proposed budget. It is a good idea to pray before you begin. Commit your finances to God and determine to work together in a financial agreement. It may take several hours of your time to complete, but maintaining your budget will be much less time consuming.

Instructions

Record the known or estimated monthly dollar figure for each category on the budget sheet. (We've included two blank sheets for you.) The definitions of the categories are listed below to help you determine the scope of each one. The completed example on page 46 will serve as a guideline.

Tithe: List your regular support (tithe) to your church (anything over 10% may be listed under the *Giving* category).

Tax: List federal, state and county taxes.

Investment: List any money invested for future care of your family (IRA's, retirement programs, home savings, etc).

Mortgage/Rent: List mortgage payment or rent payment.

Housing Maintenance: If you own your home, estimate monthly maintenance costs.

Utilities: List your monthly utility costs.

Telephone: Estimate your monthly phone bill.

Food & Supplies: Include food (work and school lunches), drug store supplies, department store sundries (toiletries, laundry).

Clothing: Estimate a monthly budget.

Autos: List auto payment(s) and the cost of insurance, driver's licenses, vehicle registration, gas, and maintenance.

Medical/Dental: Include health insurance payments and money spent for medicines, medical/dental/optical checkups.

Gifts: List monthly expenses for gifts (birthday, wedding, etc).

Stationery: Estimate the cost of postage and stationery.

Dining: List restaurant meals eaten out.

Travel/Vacation: List weekend travel and yearly vacation expenses.

Recreation/Entertainment: List money spent for family activities and sporting events (swimming, bowling, movies, football games, etc).

Miscellaneous: List expenses not covered above, college loans, marriage seminars, periodical subscriptions, life insurance, and personal debt.

Giving: List missionary support and special offerings.

Savings: List money set aside for emergencies. Indicate withdrawals with brackets ( ).

When the monthly budget amounts are completed, compute the totals. First, work from left to right adding up annual totals for each category. The annual totals added together, excluding income, can be more than, equal to, or less than the total annual income. Figure the average monthly total for each category by dividing each annual total by twelve.

Personal Finances Budget Sheet

Category percentages that may be helpful in preparing a budget.

Category	January	February	March	April	May	June	July	August	September	October	November	December	Annual Total	Average Monthly Total
Income														
Tithe														
Federal Tax 16.9%														
State Tax 2.1%														
County Tax 1%														
Investment FICA														
Mortgage														
Rent														
Housing Maintenance														
Electricity														
Heat														
Water														
Sewer														
Disposal														
Telephone														
Food & Supplies														
Clothing														
Auto Payment/Lease														
Auto Gas/Oil														
Auto Insurance														
Auto License/Reg.														
Auto Maintenance														
Medical/Dental														
Gifts														
Stationery														
Dining														
Travel/Vacation														
Rec/Entertainment														
Miscellaneous														
Education														
Subscriptions														
Life Insurance														
Debt														
Giving														
Savings														
Cumulative Savings														

Category percentages (left column):
- 10% — Tithe
- 20% — Federal Tax 16.9%, State Tax 2.1%, County Tax 1%
- 8% — Investment FICA
- 21% — Housing Maintenance, Electricity, Heat, Water, Sewer, Disposal, Telephone
- 11% — Food & Supplies
- 2.2% — Clothing
- 9.9% — Auto Insurance, Auto License/Reg., Auto Maintenance
- 2.5% — Medical/Dental
- 2% — Gifts
- .5% — Stationery
- 3.1% — Dining, Travel/Vacation, Rec/Entertainment
- 6.7% — Miscellaneous, Education, Subscriptions, Life Insurance, Debt
- 1.1% — Giving
- 2% — Savings

Husband and wife are paid weekly on Fridays. *Indicates the months with 5 Fridays. Husband earns $7.50 per hour, 40 hours per week and the wife earns $5.50 per hour, 20 hours per week. They have no children.

Personal Finances Budget Sheet

Category percentages that may be helpful in preparing a budget.

%	Category	January	February	March	April	May	June	July	August	September	October	November	December	Annual Total	Average Monthly Total
	Income														
10%	Tithe														
	Federal Tax 16.9%														
20%	State Tax 2.1%														
	County Tax 1%														
8%	Investment FICA														
	Mortgage														
	Rent														
	Housing Maintenance														
	Electricity														
21%	Heat														
	Water														
	Sewer														
	Disposal														
	Telephone														
11%	Food & Supplies														
2.2%	Clothing														
	Auto Payment/Lease														
	Auto Gas/Oil														
9.9%	Auto Insurance														
	Auto License/Reg.														
	Auto Maintenance														
2.5%	Medical/Dental														
2%	Gifts														
.5%	Stationery														
	Dining														
3.1%	Travel/Vacation														
	Rec/Entertainment														
6.7%	Miscellaneous														
	Education														
	Subscriptions														
	Life Insurance														
	Debt														
1.1%	Giving														
2%	Savings														
	Cumulative Savings														

Husband and wife are paid weekly on Fridays. *Indicates the months with 5 Fridays. Husband earns $7.50 per hour, 40 hours per week and the wife earns $5.50 per hour, 20 hours per week. They have no children.

Three Parts of Man

Read and study together.

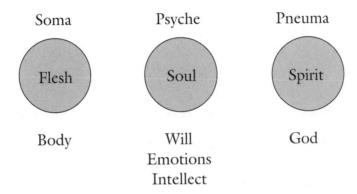

Soma	Psyche	Pneuma
Flesh	Soul	Spirit
Body	Will	God
	Emotions	
	Intellect	

We know God as Father, Son, and Holy Spirit. Just as God is three in one, so is man whom He created. God has designed man with flesh, our body which will return to the dust of the earth (Gen. 3:19); soul, our will, emotions, and intellect (Ezek. 18:4; Matt. 10:28); and spirit (Gen. 1:27; 1 Thess. 5:23; Heb. 11:12).

This illustration will help to clarify God's design for marriage. If the marriage is built in the fleshly realm (the lust of the eyes, the lust of the flesh—1 John 2:16) it will not endure. Before long this marriage will experience tremendous difficulty. There is much more to a relationship than the physical act of sex.

When a marriage is built in the soul realm, it may also be short-lived. Two college graduates may be able to communicate on a very intelligent level, but this alone will not be enough to sustain the relationship. If a marriage decision was made out of a strong will or during an "emotional high," this too will soon fade.

However, when a marriage is built in the spiritual realm, it is off to a powerful start. The Bible clearly indicates that God the Father, God the Son, and God the Spirit agree as one (1 John 5:8). Amos 3:3 states, "Can two walk together, unless they are *agreed*?" This agreement must first take place in the spiritual realm. Now let's look together at Matthew 18:19.

"Again, I [Jesus] say to you that if two of you on earth *agree* concerning anything that they ask, it will be done for them by My Father in heaven." (Emphasis on the word *agree* is ours.) The Bible indicates that when the two of you agree it will be done. This is why a marriage built in the spiritual realm is so powerful.

If the two of you agree in prayer about a financial need, a physical need, an emotional need, or a spiritual need according to God's will, it will be done. There is power in your agreement. Consequently, the key is to not argue about the need but to pray and agree.

When a marriage is built in the spirit, all of hell cannot touch it. The enemy loves to attack our flesh and our soul, but when we are built up in the spirit we need not give him any ground.

Discuss areas in which you have discovered the power of agreement with your spouse. _____

_____

_____

_____

_____

Prayerfully list some areas in which you feel agreement still needs to be actively pursued. _____

_____

_____

_____

_____

Forgiveness: A Final Word

Jesus taught us in Matthew 6:14–15 that if we forgive others, the Lord will forgive us. You choose whether or not to forgive. As someone appropriately said, forgiveness is God's medicine. You will feel at times that the person who has angered you does not deserve forgiveness. Jesus did not say to forgive only those who deserve forgiveness. Forgiveness releases you, as well as the one who wronged you.

Forgiveness is an important ingredient in a marriage. Anyone in close relationship with another is bound to encounter times of stress and frustration. It is at these times that we may say the wrong thing or behave in the wrong way. The following is a practical, step-by-step, scripturally based process for forgiveness.

This exercise completes the formal postmarital training. However, it is our hope that you will continue accountability, prayer, Bible study, and an ongoing desire to grow in your relationship with Christ and with each other. God bless you in your call together.

Seven Steps to Forgiveness

1. Choose to forgive.

Forgiveness begins with a simple decision that, in Jesus' name, we will obey God and forgive those who have hurt us.

"And be kind to one another, tenderhearted, forgiving one another, even as God in Christ forgave you" (Eph. 4:32).

Jesus made it clear in Matthew 18:35 that this decision to forgive is to be from the heart. We are to forgive wholeheartedly, not holding back or keeping any resentments.

But what about feelings? Here are some helps in dealing with them.

Forgiveness starts not with feelings, but with a decision. You don't need to wait for the right feeling before deciding to forgive. Instead, you can forgive!

You can immediately choose to forgive from your heart, and God will recognize that. Verbalize this decision—by faith confess aloud, "In Jesus' name I forgive ——————." When you have done this, your feelings will be worked out. God will see to it!

Be alert! The devil may try to bring some feelings of resentment back into your life. You do not need to feel guilty about these temptations, but you do need to deal with them. Since you have already made your choice, you need to stand firm on having already forgiven that person in Jesus' name (1 Peter 5:8–10).

When that feeling of resentment comes back, say to yourself, "I did forgive! I dealt with that." Eventually when you remember that sad experience, it will be with the happy thought, "That's all over." Herein lies the healing of memories.

2. Confess your sin to God.

Unforgiveness is sin against God. It is disobedience to His command to forgive others even as God has forgiven us (Eph. 4:32). Even more, God desires for all people to know forgiveness; He sent His Son, Jesus, to die in order to make that possible. Unforgiveness can stop people from experiencing God's forgiveness. Unforgiveness is a terrible sin against God.

Yet God is always ready to forgive those who call on Him (Ps. 86:5). So accept your unforgiveness as sin and confess it to God. Do you know what He does then?

"If we confess our sins, He is faithful and just to forgive us our sins and to cleanse us from all unrighteousness" (1 John 1:9). (This confessing implies naming our sins one by one.)

"He who covers his sins will not prosper, but whoever confesses and forsakes them will have mercy" (Prov. 28:13).

How can we be sure we are forgiven? By God's Word! He very clearly says: "For if you forgive men their trespasses, your heavenly Father will also forgive you" (Matt. 6:14).

"If we confess our sins, He is faithful and just to forgive us our sins and to cleanse us from all unrighteousness" (1 John 1:9).

Yet sometimes you still doubt that you are really forgiven. There is one more thing that you need to do. Receive God's forgiveness, accepting it just as you would accept a gift someone gave to you. How is this possible? Listen to what the Apostle Paul said:

"Now then, we are ambassadors for Christ, as though God were pleading through us: we implore you on Christ's behalf, be reconciled to God. For He made Him who knew no sin to be sin for us, that we might become the righteousness of God in Him" (2 Cor. 5:20–21).

3. Ask forgiveness of those you wronged.

We are responsible to restore relationship with anyone who has anything against us (Matt. 5:23–24). Accept responsibility for the wrong you have done, and ask for the person's forgiveness. If you do not know what you did wrong, ask God to show you.

Simply ask forgiveness. Do not go into details that would do more harm than good.

If you do not have a genuine sorrow or repentance in going to that person, stop first and prayerfully ask God to show you how you hurt that person and how he may have felt. Allow God to give you a whole new understanding and sensitivity toward that person.

It is good to look right at the person when you tell him what you did wrong and ask, "Will you forgive me?" Wait for an answer. If he says, "Yes, I will forgive," this will bring a release to him also. (Regardless of his answer, by confessing your sin and asking forgiveness, you have been obedient. You can now leave the situation in God's hands.)

4. Ask God to bless the person who hurt you.

"Bless those who curse you, and pray for those who spitefully use you" (Luke 6:28).

Ask God to truly bless the person who hurt you. And as you do this, follow the example of Jesus in asking God to bless them by forgiving them!

5. Do something nice for the person who hurt you (bless them).

"Do good to those who hate you" (Luke 6:27).

"Do not be overcome by evil but overcome evil with good" (Rom. 12:21).

This could be accomplished by complimenting that person, baking some cookies, fixing a car, or babysitting. Ask God and He will show some act that will be meaningful to that person.

6. Accept that person the way he is, even if he is wrong.

Don't defend what he does, but defend him. You do not necessarily need to approve of what he is doing, but treat him with dignity, respect, love, and kindness anyway.

"Therefore receive one another, just as Christ also received us, to the glory of God" (Rom. 15:7).

7. Look at that person through the eyes of faith and believe God to change him.

Do not concentrate on areas of weakness, sin, or irritation. Rather, concentrate on seeing that person as God wants him to be. Believe that God will answer your prayers for that person (1 John 5:14–15). Follow Abraham's example and by faith see things that are not as they appear (Rom. 4:16–21). Begin to think and speak positively about that person (1 Cor. 13:7). Love "believes all things, hopes all things."

Summary

Here is a quick, personalized summary of these seven steps to forgiveness:

1. In Jesus' name, I choose to forgive those who have hurt me.

2. I will confess my sins to God, especially the terrible sin of unforgiveness. (And, by faith, I will receive God's forgiveness and cleansing.)
3. I will, as God directs me, ask others for forgiveness for the wrongs I have done to them. (And I will make restitution as needed.)
4. From now on, I will ask God to bless the one who has hurt me.
5. I, too, will bless that person, doing kind, helpful things for him.
6. I will accept him and treat him with love and respect.
7. I will look at that person through eyes of faith, and trust God to work in him.

List below any persons that you know you need to forgive. This list may include your spouse, a parent, a friend, a coworker, someone from your childhood, yourself, or perhaps even God.

_____

_____

_____

_____

_____

_____

Pray over this list individually or with your spouse and be accountable to your postmarital counselors. Be sure to look back over the seven steps and see if you have completed them for each person you need to forgive.

Adapted from *Seven Steps to Forgiveness.* Copyright © 1985 by Norman and Betty Charles. Used by permission of Abundant Living Ministries.

Appendices

Appendix A

Are You on Schedule?

Check this wedding timetable.
- Discuss possible engagement with parents. Be sure of their approval.
- Discuss possible engagement with those in spiritual authority, i.e., pastor, associate pastor, premarital counselor(s).
- Seek counsel concerning an appropriate time frame for the wedding.

The Bride's Timetable

Six Months to a Year before the Wedding

- Discuss and set wedding budget with parents. Include groom and his parents in discussions if they are sharing costs.
- Review, evaluate, and comparison shop for wedding sites. Select a wedding date, time, and place as soon as possible.
- Start making guest list.
- Plan color scheme for ceremony and reception.
- Select and order wedding dress.
- Choose attendants for wedding and invite them to participate.

- Reserve caterer and musicians.
- Register at one or more stores for china, silverware, and other household items.
- Purchase wedding ring for groom.

Three Months before the Wedding

- Complete guest lists and check for duplication.
- Order invitations and enclosure cards as well as personal stationery (for thank-you notes and future use).
- Address invitations.
- Choose wedding party attire for bridesmaids' dresses and mothers of bride and groom. Groom and male attendants should select outfits.
- Shop for trousseau.
- Hire photographer and/or video cameraman to record wedding day.
- Arrange for bridal portrait, if being taken ahead of time.
- Arrange for tests for marriage license, if required.
- Discuss ceremony and music with appropriate personnel.
- Finalize reception plans.
- Order wedding cake.
- Order wedding flowers for bridal party, ceremony, and reception.

One Month before the Wedding

- Mail invitations.
- Check guidelines for newspaper wedding announcements. Prepare the announcement and send in when required.
- Have final dress fitting.
- Have wedding portrait taken.
- Choose and order gifts for attendants.
- Select gift for groom.
- Arrange accommodations for out-of-town relatives and attendants.
- Plan bridesmaids' party, if giving one.

Three Weeks before the Wedding

- Get marriage license with fiancé.
- Arrange transportation for bridal party to ceremony.

- Discuss details of wedding and reception with photographer (or video camera operator).
- Remind each member of the wedding party of the date, time, and place of rehearsal and wedding.

One Week before the Wedding

- Begin honeymoon packing.
- Give or go to the bridesmaids' party; present gifts to attendants at brides-maids' party or rehearsal dinner.
- Provide final estimate of number of reception guests to caterer.
- Check on final details with florist, photographer, and musicians.
- Arrange to move wedding gifts and personal belongings to your new home.

The Groom's Timetable

Six Months before the Wedding

- Order engagement and wedding rings for bride.
- Start guest list.
- Select best man and other attendants (usually one usher for each fifty guests).
- Discuss honeymoon plans with bride and begin making arrangements.

Three Months before the Wedding

- Complete guest list; make sure addresses are correct.
- Consult with bride about appropriate dress for you and male attendants.
- Complete honeymoon plans and purchase tickets.
- Consult with bride on flowers for bridal bouquet and going-away corsage (usually paid for by groom).
- Arrange accommodations for out-of-town relatives and ushers.

One Month before the Wedding

- Pick up wedding ring; check on engraving.
- Help plan rehearsal dinner if your parents are hosting.
- Select gift for bride.
- Choose gifts for attendants. Make sure documents are in order (legal, medical, and religious).

Three Weeks before the Wedding

- Get marriage license.
- Check on arrangements for bachelor dinner if you are giving one.
- Arrange for transportation to and from reception site.

One Week before the Wedding

- Remind best man and ushers of rehearsal time and place.
- Present gifts to attendants.
- Explain any special seating needs to head usher.
- Get wedding clothes and going-away clothes ready.

Appendix B

Who Pays for What?

Bride

- Wedding ring for the groom
- A wedding gift for the groom
- Gifts for the bridal attendants
- Personal stationery
- Medical examination and blood test
- Accommodations for out-of-town attendants

Groom

- The bride's engagement and wedding rings
- A wedding gift for the bride
- Gifts for the best man and ushers
- Groom's wedding attire
- Bride's bouquet and going-away corsage
- Mothers' corsages
- Boutonnieres for attendants and fathers
- Medical examination and blood test
- Marriage license
- Clergyman's fee

- Honeymoon expenses
- Bachelor dinner (if not given by the best man, optional)

Bride's family

- Engagement party (optional)
- Ceremony cost: location, music, rentals, and all related expenses
- Entire cost of reception: food, beverages, entertainment, rental items, decorations, wedding cake
- Bride's wedding attire and accessories
- Wedding gift for the couple
- Wedding invitations, announcements, and mailing costs
- Bridesmaids' bouquets
- Transportation for bridal party from bride's home to the site of ceremony
- Bridesmaids' luncheon
- Photography (groom's parents may pay for the pictures they would like)
- Personal wedding attire
- Floral decorations

Groom's family

- Rehearsal dinner party
- Personal wedding attire
- Travel and accommodations for groom's family
- Wedding gift for the couple
- Special items they may wish to purchase: toasting goblets, ring pillow, etc.
- Any general expenses they may wish to contribute to

Appendix C

Birth Control

Children are a unique gift from God and provide a lifetime of blessing. The psalmist said, "Behold, children are a heritage from the Lord, and the fruit of the womb is a reward. . . . Happy is the man that hath his quiver full of them" (Ps. 127:3, 5). God has given us the ability to combine genes and see another human being with certain traits come forth. This "fruit" is the "heritage" that provides the "reward" of blessing to this new union.

God encouraged us in Genesis 1:28 to "be fruitful, and multiply; fill the earth." Therefore, marriage includes procreation. Some teach that a "quiver" contained five arrows. God leaves the decision concerning the number of children you give birth to up to you. Most Christians use some method of birth control, so we include a section on the subject. Each couple should pray and agree concerning the number of children they can train to serve God.

The following information was written by Scott Jackson, M.D. It is not all-inclusive but does provide a concise look at several methods of birth control. As a couple, pray, consult your physician, and educate yourselves. You may want to ask your doctor directly, "Is this method of birth control abortive?"

There are certain types of oral contraceptives which would be considered abortive. Again, we recommend that you discuss this important matter with your family physician or contact the National Right to Life, Suite 402, 4197th Street, N.W., Washington, D.C. 20004; telephone (202) 626-8800 with any questions.

Options

Oral Contraceptives

Ovulation is directed by hormones, mainly estrogen and progesterone. Oral contraceptives consist of man-made versions of these hormones. They work to prevent the ovaries from producing eggs. Also, they help prevent sperm from reaching an egg. Several types of oral contraceptives exist with different levels of hormones. They also are available in 21-day or 28-day packs. Your doctor can determine which is right for you. Oral contraceptives are the most effective birth control method. Side effects are rare but can include headaches, weight gain, breast tenderness, and mid-cycle bleeding. There is a higher chance of blood clots or vascular disease, especially if one smokes while on the pill. The use of oral contraceptives must be monitored by a physician and must include yearly pap tests.

Diaphragm

The diaphragm is a soft rubber or latex cup that is inserted into the vagina to cover the cervix. It works as a barrier to sperm and is used with spermicidal jelly or cream which kills sperm before they enter the uterus and fertilize the egg. The diaphragm will need to be fitted by your physician. He will instruct you on how to insert it and how to apply the spermicide. The diaphragm is highly effective if properly used. It must be inserted prior to intercourse each time. Afterwards, it can be cleaned with soap and water. The diaphragm should be replaced every two years.

Spermicides

Spermicides kill sperm so that none can enter the uterus and fertilize an egg. They consist of jellies, cream, foam, or suppositories. When used with a diaphragm, they can be highly effective. Some use foam or suppositories without a diaphragm. They can be obtained without a prescription and are rather inexpensive. However, their effectiveness in birth control is not as high as the two previous methods mentioned.

Cervical Cap

The cervical cap is a smaller version of the diaphragm. It consists of a slightly thicker rubber and is filled with spermicidal jelly or cream. It should be fitted by your physician and must be rechecked yearly. The cervical cap is applied at the time of each intercourse.

Condoms

The condom is a thin shield of latex that fits over the man's penis. It traps expelled semen during intercourse, preventing sperm from fertilizing an egg. The condom should be applied to the erect penis before intercourse. Afterward, he should withdraw immediately to prevent leakage. Condoms should be used in combination with spermicidal suppositories, jelly, cream, or foam as a backup form of birth control in case of leakage or breakage. Condoms, in general, are not as effective in birth control as the pill or diaphragm.

Contraceptive Sponges

The contraceptive sponge is a small, disposable, round, spermicide-containing sponge, which can be purchased over-the-counter. Use of the sponge can be fairly expensive because a new sponge must be used each time a couple has intercourse. Water is applied to the sponge, and it is inserted over the cervix. It does provide 24-hour protection and is about as effective as the diaphragm, except in women who have already had children.

Intrauterine Device

The IUD is a small plastic or metal device that is placed by a physician inside the uterus through the opening in the cervix. The IUD is highly effective in birth control. It is thought to work by preventing the fertilized egg from implanting on the uterine wall or by blocking the sperm from reaching the egg. Some have felt that the IUD contradicts Christian values by possibly causing a type of abortion since the egg may already be fertilized at the time it is prevented from implanting on the uterine wall. The IUD must be checked at least annually and must be changed regularly. Check with your physician for further information and guidelines that he may suggest.

Natural Family Planning

Natural family planning or "the rhythm method" utilizes the fact that fertilization is most likely to occur just before, during, or after ovulation. It is the least effective birth control method since even the most regular cycles can vary from month to month. The woman can monitor her ovulation schedule by checking her body temperature every morning and plotting it on a calendar for several months. She usually sees a slight rise in temperature during ovulation. Usually a pattern occurs, alerting the couple to avoid intercourse during the most fertile days. Most find that ovulation occurs fourteen days before the start of the next menstrual period. Another way of determining ovulation is cervical mucus charting which involves observing a sample of mucus from the vagina daily. The mucus becomes clear, elastic, and slippery during ovulation.

Appendix D

Honeymoon Precautions

Sometimes new brides, especially those who are virgins, develop some painful, if not embarrassing, symptoms during or shortly after the honeymoon. We have included short descriptions of "honeymoon cystitis" and vaginitis as preventative information for the new bride and groom.

Cystitis

The urethra or tube draining urine from the bladder can be easily bruised, especially if not enough lubrication is provided for the penis to be inserted into the vagina. "Honeymoon cystitis" can result in bladder pain, bloody urine, or burning upon urination. Bruising of the urethra allows bacteria to grow in the urine stream causing an infection. This can be easily cured with antibiotic therapy and drinking plenty of fluids. Repeated attacks can sometimes be prevented by urinating after each time of intercourse.

Vaginitis

Vaginitis, inflammation of the vagina, may have a host of causes. Usually, the woman will experience burning or unusual vaginal discharge. Sometimes painful intercourse results. She should seek medical attention in the event of any suspicion of vaginitis. There are over-the-counter preparations which promote effective cures; however, these should be used only under the recommendations of a physician. Some types of vaginitis can be passed from wife to husband and may require antibiotics for both partners.

Appendix E

Resource List

Additional books for instruction and reading pleasure recommended by the authors:

Backus, Dr. William. *Telling Yourself the Truth.* Minneapolis: Bethany House Publishers, 1980.

Burkett, Larry. *Answers to Your Family's Financial Questions.* Pamona, California: Focus on the Family, 1987.

Bustanoby, André. *Just Talk to Me: Talking and Listening for a Happier Marriage.* Grand Rapids, Michigan: Zondervan Publishing House, 1981.

Cole, Edwin Louis, *Maximized Manhood.* Springdale, Pennsylvania: Whitaker House, 1982.

Crabb, Dr. Larry. *The Marriage Builder: A Blueprint for Couples and Counselors.* Grand Rapids, Michigan: Pyranee Books, 1982.

Exley, Richard. *The Rhythm of Life: Putting Life's Priorities in Perspective.* Tulsa, Oklahoma: Honor Books, 1987.

Seamonds, David A. *Healing for Damaged Emotions: Recovering from Memories That Cause Pain*. Wheaton, Illinois: Victor Books, 1981.

Smalley, Gary. *If Only He Knew: A Valuable Guide to Knowing, Understanding, and Loving Your Wife*. Grand Rapids, Michigan: Pyranee Books, 1988.

————. *Love Is a Decision: Ten Proven Principles to Energize Your Marriage and Family*. Dallas: Word Publishing, 1989.

Wheat, Ed, M.D. *Intended for Pleasure: Sexual Technique and Sexual Fulfillment in Marriage*. Old Tappan, New Jersey: Fleming H. Revell Co., 1977.

————. *Love Life for Every Married Couple*. Grand Rapids, Michigan: Pyranee Books, 1980.

Williams, Pat and Jill. *Keep the Fire Glowing: How a Loving Marriage Builds a Loving Family*. Old Tappan, New Jersey: Fleming H. Revell Co., 1986.

Wright, H. Norman. *Understanding the Man in Your Life*. Dallas: Word Publishing, 1987.

Appendix F

Course Evaluation

Your input concerning this material would be very helpful to us. Please complete the following questionnaire and mail it to this address:

> *Called Together*
> Steve and Mary Prokopchak
> 1924 West Main Street
> Ephrata, PA 17522

1. What effect has the *Called Together* premarital training program had on your marriage preparation?

   _____very strong effect _____strong effect _____moderate effect
   _____little effect _____no effect

2. What was the most important information that you received from the *Called Together* premarital training?

3. What areas needed more emphasis?

4. What areas needed less emphasis?

5. What was it that you enjoyed/appreciated most about your premarital counselors?

6. What was it that you least enjoyed/appreciated about your premarital counselors?

7. If you were able to change the *Called Together* counseling program, what additions or deletions would you make?

8. How long did it take you to complete premarital training?

_____ 4-6 weeks   _____ 11-12 weeks
_____ 7-10 weeks   _____ other (please specify)

9. Do you have any other recommendations or suggestions for the *Called Together* counseling program?

Counselor's Guide

Counselor's Guide

Where can an engaged couple find clear, biblical premarital instruction? Did you and your spouse participate in any type of premarital counseling? We encourage you to take time to answer the following questions:

1. Did you and your spouse receive premarital counseling?
2. Did your pastor require that you have premarital counseling?
3. Who administered your premarital counseling?
4. How many sessions of counseling did you attend?
5. What were the topics discussed in each session?
6. Did you receive any homework assignments? Did you complete the assignments?
7. Were you assigned any books to read? If yes, what were the titles of the books?
8. Did you complete any personality assessments or other tests?
9. Was the sexual relationship discussed to your satisfaction?
10. Were finances discussed in detail?
11. Rate your premarital counseling (1 = inadequate, 10 = excellent)

12. How much effect did your premarital counseling have upon your marriage relationship? (1 = very little; 10 = very much)
13. Did you receive any postmarital counseling?

While training local church couples to give premarital counseling, we asked some of these same questions. Many couples struggled to remember whether or not they had participated in premarital counseling. Some couples could not remember what content had been covered in their counseling.

One couple shared that they met with a psychologist for two premarital sessions. When asked why they attended only two sessions, they replied, "That's all we could afford." This is a sad testimony to where the church has been in relation to training couples for marriage.

Where does a couple go for marriage training? The answer is obvious: to the church. Most couples desire to have a church wedding. However, many pastors have shied away from in-depth premarital counseling sessions for several reasons. One reason is the time commitment involved. Most pastors have tight schedules. Sadly, a second reason is the lack of comprehensive materials available to pastors.

Another question for pastors to consider is this: What is your philosophy concerning premarital education? Your philosophy will determine your premarital counseling process and the type of curriculum you will use.

Called Together is unique in that it is administered couple to couple. We have successfully trained committed Christian couples rather than busy pastors to administer the pre- and postmarital instruction. They have committed themselves to work with a premarital couple for six or more sessions. This time frame allows for a quality relationship to develop, which continues through the postmarital sessions. Couples who want to be married at our church are required to participate in premarital counseling. Throughout the counseling process, they are challenged and encouraged. As the counselor couple studies the premarital material, they also become vulnerable and accountable to the couple whom they are counseling.

Let us share some reasons why we believe pre- and postmarital counseling is extremely important:

- Marriage was designed by God. We need to do our best to see each marriage built upon a proper foundation.

- Premarital counseling will expose potential problem areas. As these problem areas are exposed, they can be lovingly dealt with. This is preventative counseling at its best.

- Premarital counseling will build the faith of the couple or it will reveal to the couple that they are, in fact, not called together.

    Note: We do not refuse premarital counseling to anyone. However, we also make no promises to marry anyone. What we do, we must do in faith (Rom. 14:23).

- Premarital counseling can be provocative and challenging.

- Premarital counseling helps the couple to get their heads "out of the clouds," to face differences and reality.

- Postmarital counseling is a check-up and review, their first oil change, so to speak. Postmarital counseling within the first year of marriage provides opportunities for guidance, feedback, and prayer and a healthy environment in which to discuss troublesome areas of the marriage.

- Postmarital counseling reflects reality now that the couple has said, "I do." They now "know" one another. Faults and weaknesses have been exposed. The counseling couple can affirm strengths and encourage growth.

If we believe in strong, Christ-centered families, we must believe in and institute a thorough pre- and postmarital program.

This manual is a guide to the effective use of the *Called Together* pre- and postmarital program. *Called Together* is designed to provoke the couple to think and respond in writing. Each session will be approximately two hours long. Confidentiality on the part of both couples is essential. Disclosure is vital and details should not be discussed outside of the counseling sessions without permission.

Counselor couples must be willing to share about their marriage and provide a godly role model. They must also be willing to talk about difficult areas within the marriage relationship. They cannot be embarrassed to discuss such topics as childhood, family of origin issues, sexual foreplay, salvation, etc. Counselor couples need to be able to ask pertinent questions. Dependence upon the Spirit of God is essential. The Holy Spirit can reveal hidden areas such as family curses, previous sexual involvement; past physical, emotional, or sexual abuse; unhealthy relationships from the counselees' pasts. Counselor couples must not be afraid to confront sin in a loving manner.

The remainder of this instructional notebook will provide specific directions for each counseling session. Personalize each session according to the particular couple's needs. Pray with the couple frequently. Be sure to maintain accountability in all areas, with special focus on the couples' physical relationship while they are engaged.

God bless you as you provide thorough pre- and postmarital counseling in order to better equip the saints.

Before Session One

The following instructions will help you to initiate the premarital training efficiently and with confidence. *Called Together* is best administered couple to couple. Consequently, a relationship will develop that could carry on throughout the new marriage. Before Session One, the engaged couple should receive the *Called Together* manuals and complete the first three homework exercises as well as the Premarital Counseling Identification Data found on pages xv through xviii. They should receive a copy of the Pre-marriage Awareness Inventory. This inventory is designed to identify the areas in a couple's relationship which are in greatest need of discussion. This 105-item survey is available through Shepherd's Staff, 346 Chestnut Street, St. Paul, Minnesota 35107.

Important: all of these items are to be completed and turned in to you, the counselor, before Session One. This will facilitate your review of their recorded answers and help prepare you to personalize the counseling sessions according to their needs as a couple. Assignments for the remaining sessions should also be completed and in your possession *before* the corresponding session.

It may be advisable to meet with the couple before initiating any premarital sessions. During this time you should assess their relationship with God and whether or not God is calling you to be involved in their premarital training. For those who are equipped not only to give premarital training, but also to perform the actual marriage ceremony, it would be advisable to tell the couple that being involved in premarital counseling is no guarantee that you will perform the wedding ceremony. Performing the actual ceremony is something that God must give you faith for only after He has confirmed the couple and their call together.

Give copies of the books *Love Life for Every Married Couple* by Ed Wheat and *Maximized Manhood* by Edwin Louis Cole to the couple at the beginning of the premarital counseling. A copy of the book *The Act of Marriage* by Tim and Beverly LaHaye can be given when you sense that it is appropriate for the couple to begin reading about sexual relations. The books should be read by the counselees before the last session of counseling. (Again, an exception may be *The Act of Marriage* book. Some couples have expressed difficulty with their physical relationship due to the explicit nature of the material covered in this book.)

A three-part video entitled *Before You Say I Do* is an excellent tape series for the couple to view on their own while receiving premarital instruction. In this series, Norm Wright discusses communication, Larry Burkett discusses finances, and Tim and Beverly LaHaye share about the sexual relationship. This video can be rented or purchased at most Christian book stores.

In Appendix A and Appendix B you will find helpful resources for the couple to use in the planning stage of the wedding. Birth control information is available in Appendix C, and Appendix D offers honeymoon precautions.

Introduction to the Premarital Course

A. Goals of Premarital Training:
    1. To introduce the couple to God's institution of marriage
    2. To thoroughly prepare a couple for marriage

B. Sub-goals of Premarital Training:
    1. To assist the couple in taking an honest look at themselves
    2. To help the couple in evaluating their present relationship
    3. To improve communication skills
    4. To aid in the development of financial skills and financial accountability
    5. To provide accurate and appropriate information in the area of sexual relations
    6. To aid the couple in ceremony planning.

C. Objectives of Premarital Training will be met:
    1. By attending at least five premarital sessions and one marriage ceremony planning session
    2. By studying scriptural marriage concepts
    3. By observing aspects of marriage exemplified by couple counselors
    4. By completing reading and writing assignments
    5. By completing evaluation materials
        a. Pre-marriage Awareness Inventory
        b. Personality Profile
    6. By participating in open discussion, Bible study, and prayer

About Me

In order to prepare couples for a God-honoring and personally satisfying relationship in marriage, an initial marital readiness assessment should be conducted. To assist the counselor, spiritual overviews of both individuals and "About Me" worksheets are included in the assignments for Session One. Discuss the intent of these worksheets in Session One in order to help determine potential spiritual conflict or compatibility. Responses to the "About Me" questions will reveal a wealth of individual reactions to anger, fear, guilt, etc. Realistically speaking, many couples never see beyond the "nice" side of their fiancé. In order to be prepared to face difficulties or conflicts in marriage, couples should be better informed about the "other" side of their fiancé.

Session One is the time to administer the Biblical Personal Profile or a personality tool which you have been trained to use. For more information on the Biblical Personal Profile, you can write or call the authors of *Called Together.* You may give the results to the couple in Session Two or throughout the premarital sessions. However you choose to use this tool, be considerate and wise when revealing the information to the couple.

A scriptural review of love should be included in Session One. The exercise A Biblical Concept of Love offers a basis for this discussion. Wedding timetables found in Appendix A are included to assist the couple in making plans for their wedding and a handout entitled "Who Pays for What?" Appendix B, will help clarify financial obligations.

Cover Section IV: Interests and Preferences; Section V: Personality and Relating Style; and Section IX: Religion of the Pre-marriage Awareness Inventory throughout Session One.

Remember, do not make any assumptions concerning this couple. Treat them as if they know nothing about marriage or marriage preparation even if one or both have been previously married.

For a spiritual overview, you will want to discuss the following topics and scriptures:

Salvation ....John 3:3; Romans 10:9
Sin ....Romans 3:10, 23
Lordship ....Luke 14:33

Water Baptism	Acts 2:3
The Holy Spirit	Matthew 3:11; Acts 1:8
Prayer	Luke 18:1; 1 Thessalonians 5:17
The Word	Psalm 119:11, 105; Ephesians 6:17; Hebrews 4:12
Church Attendance	Hebrews 10:25

Finally, discuss purity with the couple. Consider these four areas:

1. Seek God first (Matt. 6:33).
2. Commit yourselves to purity (1 Tim. 5:1–2).
3. Be committed to communication so as to not defraud one another (Eph. 4:15).
4. Be committed to accountability with parents, pastor, and counselors (Luke 16:1–15).

About Us

Many couples enter marriage unrealistically. God wants us to be full of faith but "wise as serpents." With the great wealth of literature, videos, and audio tapes available on the subjects of marriage, sex, finances, communication, etc., no couple should enter marriage unaware of Satan's devices to undermine and destroy relationships.

Reasons for marriage can widely vary. The exercises Reasons for Marriage and Expectations and Perceptions of Marriage help the counselor and the couple to sift through the emotional and romantic issues in order to determine the valid call of God to marriage.

Is this couple compatible in their expectations and perceptions of marriage? Potential areas of conflict could be identified as you review both sets of expectations in your counseling session. Be careful not only to point out potential problem areas but also to point the couple to scripture passages that provide answers for these possible conflicts.

Normally, engaged couples will have the following three expectations:

1. They expect that this marriage will never end in divorce.
2. They expect faithfulness and commitment from each other.
3. They expect minimal adjustments and few, if any, problems.

Be aware that when expectations are not met they can become demands. Please share some of your premarital and postmarital expectations that were not met by your partner and how you dealt with these unmet expectations.

The exercise on reactions deals with "what if" situations. Hopefully the couple will not have to face any of these situations. But what if . . . ? Use God's Word to address these situations, offering God's hope for any problem that could arise.

The following exercise provokes discussion about parents. Family of origin issues are an essential topic for premarital counseling. Does the couple have their parents' blessing? Take the time to discuss this exercise. But be aware that these questions cannot possibly cover every issue that pertains to the family of origin.

Pre-marriage Awareness Inventory Section II: Marriage Expectations; Section VI: Emotions; and Section VIII: In-laws, accompany Session Two.

Communication

Effective communication is vital to a stable, intimate, and satisfying marriage relationship. A breakdown of communication is almost always a primary cause of marital dysfunction. Ed Cole, in his book *Communication, Sex, and Money,* states that when communication stops, abnormality sets in, and the ultimate end of abnormality is death of the relationship. Just as faith dies when we refuse to communicate with our heavenly Father, so will a marriage die when a couple refuses to communicate. Ephesians 4:29–30 reveals to us that the purpose of communication is to edify, not corrupt. The Holy Spirit is grieved when we are not ministers of grace.

The varied assignments for this session cover communication extensively—nonverbal communication, communication guidelines, effective communication, scenario communication, etc.

Our communication goals include the following: to share with one another freely; to be lovingly honest about what we think and feel; to understand each other; to listen respectfully and respond appropriately; to be able to disagree and discuss our disagreements without becoming hurt or attacking one another; and to have conversation that is beneficial and uplifting.

Norm Wright, in his book *Training Christians to Counsel,* states that communication is made up of the following components:

   7% words (content)
 38% attitude (tone of voice)
 55% body language

It will be important for you to emphasize the importance of healthy communication. As you and the couple work together, you will have the opportunity to refer to unhealthy methods of communication as well as the tone of voice and body language employed by the counselees.

James 4:1–2 informs us that conflicts come from wanting something but not getting it. In order to help the couple work through possible communication difficulties, the following synopsis for conflict resolution should be helpful.

A. Decision-making is a large part of the conflict resolution process.
Ask: Who made the decisions in their families of origin?
Who will exert more influence in decision-making in this new family?
Who will be ultimately responsible for decisions made?
How has the couple been making decisions independently?
How have they been making decisions during their engagement period?
How have they escaped decision-making in the past?
(Note: Personality profile testing results may be helpful here.)

B. Take practical steps to resolve conflict. (Remember, when conflict comes, you tend to focus on yourself.)
1. Don't demand; listen (Prov. 18:13).
2. Select the right time and place (Prov. 15:23).
3. Define the problem area.
4. Define the areas of agreement and disagreement.
5. Identify your contribution to the problem—accept some responsibility.
6. Identify the behaviors you need to change.
7. Listen to the feelings of the other person.
(Feelings do not need to be factual; however, you can agree that your spouse is "feeling" this way.)
8. Find out what the Word of God says about the problem area.
9. Pray together and agree on necessary changes.

Covering the following verses will be helpful: Proverbs 13:18; 23:12; 25:12; 28:13; Isaiah 63:7; Philippians 3:13.

Premarriage Awareness Inventory Section I: Communication will be helpful with Session Three.

Finances

Conflicting ideas about finances often cause marital dysfunction. In many of the divorces filed each year in our country, complaints often involve finances.

God gives clear guidelines and principles for handling finances in His Word. Truth about finances can be found in the scriptures.

Also included in this session are assignments which will clarify personal views about finances, worksheets concerned with cost estimation, and a budget profile. Take time to cover the budget profile with the couple. Be sensitive to any potential problems in the financial area.

In Session Four, you will want to discuss financial expectations. For example, a couple may expect to purchase a new home within the first year of marriage; they may need to buy a second car or decide to replace one of their present vehicles with a newer one; they may unconsciously expect to be at the financial level of their parents or another couple whom they admire before that can be a reality. It will be important for you as counselors to confront these financial issues candidly.

Financial problems can cause stress. Couples will be tempted to use "instant credit." Take advantage of Larry Burkett's teaching in the *Before You Say I Do* video series (Tape #2). Larry will answer the credit question and address many other financial topics.

Sexual Relations

God is the creator of sex. He originated lovemaking between married partners. Sex is "a beautiful and intimate relationship shared uniquely by a husband and wife," as stated by Tim and Beverly LaHaye in their book *The Act of Marriage*.

In His Word, God has given information and directions concerning sexual relations. He doesn't consider sex an embarrassing topic. He addresses marriage in a discreet and wholesome way. As counselors, we need to follow God's lead. We need to be sources of helpful and practical information. Many couples go into marriage unprepared, naive, and sadly misinformed about sexuality and sexual relations. Many Christian marriages are lacking vitality and are less than God's best, leaving unfulfilled partners to continue without hope of change.

Homework exercises found in this session will open up discussion on attitudes and beliefs about sex, scriptural references to sex in marriage, etc. Assess the couple's abilities to express themselves about sex; are they embarrassed, fearful, disgusted, naive, or do they use inappropriate terminology? Use scripture to address any misguided attitudes. Offer practical advice for the honeymoon (see Appendix D). Reassure the couple that you will be available for counsel in the postmarital relationship.

It would be advisable to locate a sex knowledge test for this chapter of study. A book that would enable you to familiarize the couple with their sexual anatomy and with terminology relating to sex would also be helpful. (*The Act of Marriage* by Tim and Beverly LaHaye or *Intended for Pleasure* by Dr. Ed Wheat are both excellent references.) Cover Section VII in the Premarriage Awareness Inventory.

Marriage Ceremony Planning

The exercises in this section are extremely important for the premarital counselors, as well as the minister who will perform the ceremony. If you have served a couple through premarital counseling but you are not going to perform the marriage ceremony, you will need to give your input and assessment to the minister. If your assessment of this couple is that they are not prepared for marriage or if you believe that they are premature in their call together, then they must be lovingly advised.

Take special note of the exercise Saying I Do. Your emphasis should be on the spiritual union that occurs during a marriage ceremony. Please familiarize yourself with these seven areas. You may encourage the couple to discuss some of the points with their parents. After the sample ceremony, take a realistic look at the honeymoon and ask the couple some candid questions. The honeymoon is an important part of the wedding planning. Take time to walk the couple through their expectations of this event.

It is very important that the couple enjoy *each* aspect of the planning—from choosing invitations, gowns, and flowers to writing their vows and making arrangements for the honeymoon. Caution the couple not to allow themselves to become anxious or frustrated with details. This is a one-time experience, and they will be grateful for happy memories.

Called Together Postmarital Course Overview

Introduction to the Postmarital Course

A. Goals of Postmarital Training:
  1. To reinforce premarital instruction and implementation of that information
  2. To provide an assessment of the positive growth within this new marriage
  3. To focus in on specific or potential problem areas within this marriage

B. Sub-goals of Postmarital Training:
  1. To aid the couple in evaluating their present relationship
  2. To provide helpful dialogue between the newly married couple and the postmarital counselors
  3. To aid the couple in the further development of spiritual skills, communication skills, financial skills, and sexual skills

C. Objectives of Postmarital Training will be met:
  1. By attending at least two postmarital sessions
  2. By readministering the Personality Profile
  3. By reviewing appropriate premarital information
  4. By modeling/dialoguing aspects of the marriage relationship with the couple and the counselors
  5. By completing reading and writing assignments
  6. By participating in prayer and Bible study

Before Session One

A general guideline for postmarital education would be to meet with the couple at three months and nine months after the wedding. The postmarital course is designed with a minimum of two sessions in mind. You may meet with this couple as often as necessary. Note that the Counselor's Guide Areas of Review are broken down into two sessions. Discuss Spiritual Overview and Communication Overview at the three-month session. Financial Overview and Sexual Overview can be reviewed at the nine-month session.

It is assumed that you were the couple's premarital counselors. If you did not perform the premarital counseling, then have a get-acquainted session. In this meeting you will need to gather as much background information as possible. You could use your *Called Together* manual as an outline for questioning.

Require the couple to bring their *Called Together* manuals and their books *Love Life for Every Married Couple* and *The Act of Marriage* to the postmarital sessions. You will also want them to bring their personality profiles. If you are certified to administer a personality profile, you will want to readminister it to the couple and note any personality/behavior differences in their graphs. It is extremely profitable to profile the couple during the postmarital training.

We recommend that the books *If Only He Knew,* by Gary Smalley, and *The Man in Your Life,* by Norm Wright, be given to the husband and wife, respectively, at the first postmarital session and completed by the last session.

The exercises should be completed and turned in to you before the three-month counseling session. The second set of exercises are to be completed and turned in to you before the nine-month session. This will give you time to review the couple's responses and make note of specific areas to discuss.

Build upon the relationship that you established during the premarital course now in the more realistic postmarital counseling sessions. Always keep in mind that counseling couples toward a Christ-centered marriage will reach their children and generations to come. Your example, warmth, love, confrontation, empathy, and understanding translate into the act of "equipping the saints for the work of ministry" (Eph. 4:12). There is no greater ministry than serving and building the Christian family!

Areas of Review for Session One

A. Spiritual Overview:
  1. Where is the couple in their relationship with Jesus Christ? Is this couple attending a church as a family, involved in daily family devotions, involved in daily individual devotions, praying with one another, tithing, and giving to others?
  2. What are their spiritual goals (for example, being involved in short-term missions or long-term missions, leading a home fellowship group, ministering to others)?
  3. What will help to make this couple spiritually successful? Please cover the following verses with the couple:

1. Our sufficiency is in Christ:
   2 Corinthians 3:5–6—"Not that we are sufficient of ourselves to think of anything as being from ourselves, but our sufficiency is from God who also made us sufficient as ministers of the new covenant, not of the letter but of the Spirit; for the letter kills, but the Spirit gives life."

2. Being effective and productive Christians:
   2 Peter 1:5–9—"But also for this very reason, giving all diligence, add to your faith virtue, to virtue knowledge, to knowledge self-control, to self-control perseverance, to perseverance godliness, to godliness brotherly kindness, and to brotherly kindness love. For if these things are yours and abound, you will be neither barren nor unfruitful in the knowledge of our Lord Jesus Christ. For he who lacks these things is shortsighted, even to blindness, and has forgotten that he was cleansed from his old sins."
   Matthew 6:21—"For where your treasure is, there your heart will be also."

3. We need not fear; He holds the future:
   1 John 4:18—"There is no fear in love; but perfect love casts out fear, because fear involves torment. But he who fears has not been made perfect in love."
   Philippians 3:13; 4:6—"Brethren, I do not count myself to have apprehended; but one thing I do, forgetting those things which are behind and

reaching forward to those things which are ahead . . . Be anxious for nothing, but in everything, by prayer and supplication, with thanksgiving, let your requests be made known to God."

4. Trust and know God:
   Proverbs 3:5–6—"Trust in the LORD with all your heart, and lean not on your own understanding; in all your ways acknowledge Him, and He shall direct your paths."
   Mark 9:23—"All things are possible to him who believes."
   Jeremiah 32:27—"Behold, I am the LORD, the God of all flesh. Is there anything too hard for me?"
   Jeremiah 9:23–24—"Thus says the LORD: 'Let not the wise man glory in his wisdom, let not the mighty man glory in his might, nor let the rich man glory in his riches; but let him who glories glory in this, that he understands and knows Me, that I am the LORD, exercising lovingkindness, judgment, and righteousness in the earth, for in these I delight,' says the LORD."

5. Be a doer:
   James 1:22–23—"But be doers of the word, and not hearers only, deceiving yourselves. For if anyone is a hearer of the word and not a doer, he is like a man observing his natural face in a mirror . . ."

B. Communication Overview:
   1. Turn to pages 14–15 of the *Called Together* manual. How has the couple dealt with the expectations about which they previously wrote? Are there new areas of expectation?
   2. Review the "Practical Steps to Resolve Conflict" found in the Communication section on the counselor's instruction page along with James 4:1–2. Review Norm Wright's analysis of communication. Ask the couple to share how they have been resolving conflicts.
   3. What has the couple discovered about nonverbal communication? Are there any ways in which a spouse has experienced negative nonverbal communication? Discuss this.
   4. Review Communication Guidelines on pages 28–31.
   5. Review appropriate "Do You Discuss" questions found on page 34.

(For example, is the couple showing their feelings and attitudes, differences and hurts without anger and criticism?)

6. Assignment: Reread Chapter 11, "The Secret of Staying in Love" (especially for newlyweds), in the book *Love Life for Every Married Couple* by Dr. Ed Wheat.

Note: Are you accountable in the above areas? Be certain that your marriage is a Christ-centered, positive example to the young couple you are counseling.

Areas of Review for Session Two

C. Financial Overview:

1. Review Personal Financial Views (page 38). How have the couple's premarital views changed? Cover again all fifteen questions.

2. Take the couple through a review of the scriptures found on pages 42–43. Are they walking in accordance with God's Word in the financial realm?

3. Is the couple using the Personal Finances Budget Sheet found on page 46 or are they keeping records with a different tool? Ask the couple to complete a new budget sheet. They can use the line item instructions found on page 119 of the *Called Together* postmarital material.

4. Thoroughly review their financial status. Are they tithing? Do they have concrete places in which to invest for their future (e.g., IRA, retirement, real estate)? Do they live in a high rent area? Is their rent within their budget? Carefully look over the utilities. How much is their monthly telephone bill? Are long distance calls within reason? Has the couple incurred new debt? Is a vehicle payment restricting them financially? Are they spending money for date nights? Is the couple overinsured/underinsured? Are they tithing (giving)? Is the couple saving for annual or semi-annual bills? Are their present bills current?

5. Question whether this couple is walking in financial agreement. Are they accountable to one another in their spending? Do they give one another an allowance? If there is a financial need are they willing to trust God to see that need met?

6. Can this couple live on the husband's salary or are they depending upon the wife's income as well? Discuss this area thoroughly along with their financial goals. Ask the couple how their goals may change when children arrive.

7. Pray for God's blessing on their finances. Share with them that God is their provider. Their ultimate source is not their job, the bank, the church, or their parents.

Note: Keep in mind that as an older, wiser couple you can help hold this younger couple accountable with their finances, if they wish. A review of their financial status and financial goals will indicate how realistic this couple is in relation to their income and expenditures.

D.Sexual Overview:
1. Go over appropriate "Questions for Discussion" found on pages 52–53. (questions 2, 4, 5, 6, and 11.)
2. What attitudes or beliefs about sex have surfaced since the wedding night? (See page 54 as a guideline.)
3. What sexual complications has the couple encountered? Are they both experiencing orgasm during intercourse? Are they free to communicate their sexual needs with one another?
4. Thoroughly review Ed Wheat's B.E.S.T. acronym found on pages 55–56.
5. Thoroughly review "A Creative Plan" found on pages 57–59. (*Note:* Encourage the couple to listen to Dr. Ed Wheat's *Sex Techniques* tapes. This series of two 90-minute cassettes focuses specifically upon the area of physical unity within marriage.)
6. Does the couple have any questions concerning birth control? See Appendix C. Have their plans for having children changed now that they are married?
7. A second series of two 90-minute cassette tapes by Dr. Ed Wheat is also recommended. This series, entitled "Love Life," offers personal counsel and practical insights on the principles of building love within the marriage.

Assignment: Reread chapters 6, 11, 13 in Dr. Ed Wheat's book *Love Life for Every Married Couple.*

Note: Be sure to remind the couple to utilize Tim and Beverly LaHaye's book *The Act of Marriage* as a helpful reference.